VIKINGS BÓK
The Poetic Edda

Translated By

Olive Bray

Revised, with an Introduction & New Glossary By

Wolf Wickham

INTELLIGENCE RESOURCES LLC
FORT GARLAND, COLORADO, U.S.A.

Copyright © 2014, 2016 Wolf Wickham
First Edition
Second Printing
All rights reserved.

ISBN-13: 978-0615755915
ISBN-10: 0615755917
Library of Congress Control Number:
2014900775

Published by
Intelligence Resources LLC
P.O.B. 340, Fort Garland, Colorado 81133 USA
Printed in the United States of America

Adapted From the Original 1908 Work;
The Elder or Poetic Edda
Commonly Known as Sæmund's Edda
Part I. The Mythological Poems.
Edited and Translated With Introduction and Notes
By Olive Bray

CONTENTS
THE FORMING VERSES

Preface	vi
Introduction	vii
The Sayings of Grimnir	1
The Wisdom of All-Wise	9
The Words of the Mighty Weaver	14
The Words of Odin, the High One	22
The Lay of Hymir	39
The Lay of Thrym	44
The Story of Skirnir	48
Day-spring and Menglöd	54
Greybeard and Thor	64

CONTENTS
THE FORMING VERSES

The Song of Rig	71
The Lay of Hyndla	77
Baldr's Dreams	82
Loki's Mocking	85
The Wise Woman's Shorter Prophecy	95
The Wise Woman's Prophecy	97
Translators Index and Keys	106
New Glossary	127

PREFACE

What is this new Heathenism that is again challenging the spirit and values in people of northern European heritage? It is the Old Custom, far older even than the Poetic Edda.

Ironically, it is Tacitus' brief ethnographic report, known to us today as the "Germania"—written by an ancient Roman senator who was no friend of the Teutonic tribes—that is the clearest surviving source on Heathenism, together with Jacob Grimm's *Teutonic Mythology*. A few useful Sagas and a corrupted assemblage of "mythical poems" called the "Poetic Edda" are pointed out to us by historians as all that remains of our "primary sources"—the curious carcass of a mangled "barbarian" cult.

What can be gained from reconstituting this distorted corpse that was all but liquidated by Christianity and two internecine world wars? The answer, if you are of Germanic heritage or spirit is; **the return of your natural soul.**

Heathen principles do not rely upon scripture; they are carried in the genes and evolved in the minds of each new generation and individual. Still, the Poetic Edda is a vital part of our history that yields much power and wisdom.

Heathenism itself is clear, brief, and bold in concept, and deceptively deep, profound, and full in practice. It embraces self-worth based upon strength and honor, family values, and a reverence for the Holy Powers who are in us and around us. The old customs help us to discover truth and uncover the "hidden" knowledge that empowers us and evolves our constructive will in this life—and the next.

I urge you to read and understand the *New Glossary* at the end of this book before turning to the Vikings Bók. Definitions evolve and change, but truth and reality are relative constants, and while there is much need for spiritual understanding, there can be little tolerance for self-delusion. Our beliefs are based upon the realities of our multiverse and not on the blind faith of either the religious right or the universalist left.

INTRODUCTION

For nearly seventeen centuries Christianity has fought to eradicate Heathen beliefs. Today the dark fables of Middle Eastern monotheism are dying out across native Western populations, just as the Northern Way, or "Germanic Neo-paganism" is steadily reconstructing itself. This renewed Teutonic Heathenism, which evolves from our Scandinavian, German, and Anglo-Saxon heritage in the West, is once again struggling to reform our principles and our reality.

The Poetic Edda stands again, as one of the main historical vestiges of a reawakening Heathenism in the West, and by the Holy Powers it gains strength and clarity with each passing season, leading us back to its primal source.

The Poetic Edda is neither poetry, as we usually think of poetry, or Edda, although the feminine Edda aspect is given a high place of honor in every Teutonic ethno-culture. Neither was it "Sæmunds Edda," as it was briefly called, after the Christian priest (1056-1133) and once supposed editor. The Poetic Edda also had nothing to do with the well-meaning, Christianized Snorri Sturlson (1179-1241), who, in attempting to make sense of the fragmented lore, wrote—an artistic sequel that became known as the "Prose Edda"—a "manual written for poets" (Bellows, 1936), that added further corruption to the freedom loving Folk beliefs by mingling them with Christianity. Today it is unclear just how much Christian, poetic, and artistic adulteration of the indigenous Northern Way has occurred, but there is evidence that it is extensive.

In particular, the Poetic Edda is certainly not the "Codex Regius," a Latin term for the "kings book," as the manuscript was so-called in 1643 when an Icelandic Lutheran Bishop, Brynjólfur Sveinsson (1605–1675), first named the collection of Old Norse writings "Edda," credited editorship of the manuscript to its collector Sæmund "the wise," and sent it, in

Christian supplication, as a dedication to the king of Denmark —an act that could only provoke the vengeance of all noble and free Heathen Folk, its true followers and guardians.

The "mythological poems" of the "Poetic Edda" are in fact the *Forming Verses* of the *Vikings Bók*. They are the wounded remains of the old customs passed on by the native Folk, artistically inflated by Skalds, and finally written down after the ruthless Christianization of Viking culture by a rising monarchy and priesthood, before they were nearly lost in time. These Forming Verses are a witness to the near total destruction of the Heathen world view by priests, kings, and poets. But the Holy Powers speak to us through these pages, calling upon us, their descendants, to rediscover their true form in the multiverse, our world tree. It is the *primal* principles found within these verses that are the foundation for a unified Teutonic religion in our own century.

The title *Vikings Bók* honors the English word *Viking*, pronounced "*Veeking*" in Old Norse, and the Old Norse word *Bók,* meaning book, pronounced "*boke.*" The words *Vikings Bók,* written together in Old Norse, would be *Vikingabók*, pronounced "*Vee-king-a-boke.*" Unlike the academic studies of Germanic "mythology" in the past, this Vikings Bók is published as an evolving spiritual resource for seekers and followers of the Northern Way.

I could not publish this work without acknowledging the contribution of Olive Bray and what I have learned about her life. She had long vanished from popular memory by the time I discovered her translation of the Poetic Edda, even as surviving copies of her book commanded an asking price of as much as $1000.00 on the internet, and coarse reproductions were offered at $30.00. My research suggests that she came from a well-to-do English family and died at the age of 31 in 1909, the year after her work appeared.

THE FORMING VERSES

Bray said "...that old books are not true because of their age, nor old lamps beautiful, unless they can be polished anew" (i). My mandate then is to polish her work anew with this newly revised edition.

I trust that my own efforts have not disturbed either the living pulse or the meaning of the strophes. My academic background is in sociology and the humanities, not Old Norse or historical linguistics. I have made only minimal clarifications to Bray's English translation, replacing archaic words with their modern equivalents, in Heathen spirit. Essentially, terms like "art" and "thou" have now become "are" and "you," while the obsolete usage of "race" has been changed to "Folk," and so on. Bray's original footnotes have been moved from the bottom of each page to the end of each fragment. I have created a *New Glossary* at the end of the book as a stimulant for further study and for current definitions. My mission is to root out the anti-Teutonic inversion of the surviving writings and to bring them back to life again and into living Heathen hands.

The Vikings Bók is a blunt, battle tested survivor. Even in its current state it stands as a lore of courage and freedom sung of the Holy Powers and our most honored ancestors, male and female—an elemental part of the revered wisdom of the enduring Teutonic Folk—unlike the revelations of the Torah, the Bible, and the Koran of the Middle East.

The question for us to answer today as descendants of the Teutonic Tribes—as modern Germanic people, is whether we have a right to preserve our own heritage, Kindred, and territory, or whether we must surrender ourselves to universalism and internationalism. We have no choice but to stand together on our feet or to die alone on our knees. Let us resolve to uphold our own standards with strength and self-determination, tempered by moderation and held in honor.

VIKINGS BÓK

I dedicate this Vikings Bók to the living descendants of the Teutonic nations, that it may be known and understood as we advance our beliefs forward in our own age. We need to study, rather than to sanctify, what the poets have written and the skalds have sung. Now is the time to turn again to our primary principles and to revere the Holy Power within and without—born in the Folk and raised in the soul of the Free.

Let it be shown throughout the worlds that the indigenous Northern Way is a living spiritual path where a free people continue to evolve in liberty, and courage, and honor, as our ancestors have done from time immemorial. "Would you know further, and what?"

Hail the Folk!

Wolf Wickham
Intelligence Resources LLC
Fort Garland, Colorado, USA 81133-0340
June 2016

THE SAYINGS OF GRIMNIR

King Hraudung had two sons, one called Agnar and the other Geirrod. When Agnar was ten years old and Geirrod was eight the two set forth in a boat with their tackle in pursuit of small fish; but the wind drove them out to sea, and in the darkness of night they broke up by the shore. They got safely to land and came upon a cottage where they stayed the winter. The old wife fostered Agnar, and her man fostered Geirrod, and taught him wisdom. In the spring the peasant got a boat for them, and when he and the woman had brought them down to the shore he held talk apart with Geirrod. Then they put out to sea and found a fair wind, and reached their father's realm. Geirrod, who was standing in the prow, sprang on shore, and pushed the boat off, saying: "Go where a fiend may take you!" And the boat was driven off. Then he went up to the town where he was well received, and, as his father was then dead, he was made king, and became a famous man.

Odin and Frigg were sitting once on Window-Shelf, gazing out over all the world. Said Odin: "See you Agnar, your fosterling, how he begets children with a giantess in a cave? But Geirrod, my fosterling, is a king, and rules over the realm." "He is such a meat-grudger," answered Frigg, "that he starves his guests when he deems that too many are come into his halls." Odin swore that this was the greatest lie, and they wagered on the matter. Frigg sent her hand maiden Fulla to Geirrod to bid the king beware lest an enchanter, who had come into the land, should bewitch him, and she gave them this sign whereby he might be known: no dog, however fierce, would assail him. Men had lied greatly in saying that Geirrod was not hospitable, but for all that he caused a certain guest to be seized, whom the dogs would not attack. He came clad in a blue mantle, calling himself Grimnir, the Masked One, and would tell nothing else, however much they asked him. Then the king ordered him to be tortured till he should speak, and they set him in the middle between two fires, and eight nights he sat there. Geirrod's son, who was ten years old, and named Agnar after the king's brother, went up to Grimnir and gave him to drink out of a brimming horn, saying that the king had done ill to torture him so without cause; and Grimnir drank. At length, when the fire had grown so near that his cloak burned upon him, he spoke:

1. Fierce are you, fire! and far too great; flame, get you further away! my cloak is scorched though I hold it high; my mantle burns before me.
2. Eight nights have I sat between the fires, while no man offered me food, save only Agnar, the son of Geirrod, who alone shall rule the realm.
3. Blessed be you, Agnar the God of all beings shall call a blessing upon you: for one such drink you shall never more so fair a reward win.

(The Twelve Homes of the Gods.)
4. Holy is the land which lies near the world of Gods and Elves: in the Home of Strength shall the Thunderer dwell, even till the Powers perish.
5. Yew-dale is called the realm where Ull has set him a hall on high; and Elf-home that which the Gods gave Frey as tooth-gift in days of old.
6. A third home is there whose hall is thatched with silver by blessed Powers; Vala-Shelf that seat is named, which was founded in former days.
7. The fourth is Falling-brook; there, forever, the chill waves are rushing over; while day by day drink Odin and Saga, glad-hearted, from golden cups.
8. The fifth is called Glad-home, and gold-bright Valhöll, spacious, lies in its midst: there Odin shall choose his own each day of the warriors fallen in war.
9. It is easily known by all who come to visit Odin's Folk; with shafts it is raftered, with shields it is roofed, with coats of armor the benches are strewn.
10. It is easily known by all who come to visit Odin's Folk; there hangs a wolf before the western door, and an eagle hovers over.

THE FORMING VERSES

11. The sixth is Sound-home, where Thiazi lived, that fearful Jötun of old; now Skadi dwells, fair bride of Gods, in her father's former home.

12. The seventh is Broad-gleam; there has Baldr set him a hall on high, away in the land where I see are found the fewest tokens of ill.

13. The eighth is Heaven-hill; world-bright Heimdal rules over its Holy places: in that peaceful hall the watchman of Gods glad-hearted the good mead drinks.

14. The ninth is Folk-field; Freyja rules there choice of seats in the hall: one half the dead she chooses each day but half the War-father owns.

15. The tenth is Glistener pillared with gold, and also with silver roofed; there Forseti dwells near the long day through, the Judge, and soothes all strife.

16. The eleventh is Noatun; Njord in that haven has built him a hall by the sea; a prince of men, ever faultless found, he holds the high built places.

17. With brushwood grows, and with grasses high, Wood-home, Vidar's land; from his steed that son of Odin shall show him strong to avenge his sire.

(The Sky-road to Valhöll.)

18. The Thunder-flood roars, while sports the fish of the mighty Wolf therein; Overwhelming seems the flow of that stream for the host of slain to wade.

19. Halls five hundred and forty more has the Lightning-abode in its aspects, of all the high roofed houses I know, highest is that of the Thunderer.

(Valhöll.)

20. Death-barrier stands, the sacred gate, on the plain before the sacred doors; old is the lattice and few have learned how it is closed on the latch.

21. Doors five hundred, and forty more I see may be found in Valhöll; and eight hundred Chosen pass through each one when they fare to fight with the Wolf.

22. There Sooty-face boils in Sooty-flame the boar called Sooty-black; it is the best of fare, which few have heard is the chosen warriors' food.
23. Glorying, the battle-wanting Father of Hosts feeds Ravener and Greed, his wolves; but on wine alone ever Odin lives, the Weapon-famed God of war.
24. Ravens, Hugin and Munin, of Thought and Memory wing the wide world each day: I tremble for Thought, lest he come not again, yet for Memory more I fear.

(The Waters of the World.)
25. Sky-bright over Valhöll stands, the goat, who gnaws the Shelterer's boughs; she fills a bowl with the shining mead: it is a drink which runs not dry.
26. Oak-thorn over Valhöll stands, the buck, who gnaws the Shelterer's boughs; run drops from his horns into Roaring-kettle when flow all floods in the world. ...[27., 28. See notes.]
29. Kormt and Ormt and the Bath-tubs two, these must the Thunderer wade, when he fares each day to his throne of doom under Yggdrasil's ash; then Bifrost burns, the bridge of the Gods, and the mighty waters well. ...
30. Glad One, Goldy, Gleamer, Race-giant, Silvery-lock and Sinewy, Shiner, Pale-hoof, Gold-lock, Lightfoot, these are the steeds which the Gods ride, when they fare each day to their thrones of doom under Yggdrasil's ash.

(The World Tree's torments.)
31. There are three roots stretching three diverse ways from under Yggdrasil's ash: beneath the first dwells Hel, beneath the second Frost giants, and human kind beneath the third.
32. Ratatosk is the squirrel with gnawing tooth which runs in Yggdrasil's ash: he bears the eagle's words from above and to Fierce-stinger tells below.
33. There are four bucks too, who with heads thrown back gnaw the topmost boughs of the tree: Dainn the Dead One, Dvalin the Dallier, Duneyr and Dyrathror.
34. More serpents lie under Yggdrasil's ash than a witless fool would see—Goin and Moin, the offspring of Grave-monster,

THE FORMING VERSES

Grey-back and Grave-haunting worm, Weaver and Soother, I see they must ever slash the twigs of the tree.

35. Yggdrasil's ash suffers anguish more than mortal has ever known, on high gnaw bucks, it rots at the side, and Fierce-stinger slashes it beneath.

(Then cries he from the fire-torment.)

36. Would that Hrist and Mist would bear me a horn! my Valkyries, Axe and Spear-point, Bond and War-fetter, Battle and Might, Shrieker and Spear-fierce in strife; Shield-fierce, Counsel-fierce, Strength-maiden—all who bear ale to the Chosen in War.

(Sun and Earth.)

37. Early-woke, All-fleet, now must these horses wearily draw up the sun, but under their backs the Gods, gracious Powers, an iron-coolness have hid.

38. There is one called the Cooler who stands before the Sun, a shield from the shining Goddess: the mountains I see, and the stormy sea will flame if he fall from there.

39. Skoll is the wolf called who hunts the bright sun-Goddess even to the Sheltering grove; a second fares, Moon-hater, offspring of Fenrir in front of that fair bride of heaven.

40. From the flesh of Ymir the world was formed, from his blood the billows of the sea, the hills from his bones, the trees from his hair, the sphere of heaven from his skull.

41. (40) Out of his brows the joyful Powers made Middle Earth for sons of men, and out of his brains were the angry clouds all shaped above in the sky.

(The Kettle is taken off the fire in Geirrod's hall.)

42. (41) The favor of Ull and of all the Powers to him touching first the fire! For Gods can enter the homes of men when the kettle is raised from the hearth.

(The Treasures of the World.)

43. (42) Went the Wielder's sons of old to build Skidbladnir the wooden bladed, best of all ships, for the bright God Frey, ever bountiful son of Njord.

44. (43) Yggdrasil's ash, it is the best of trees, but Skidbladnir of ships, Odin of Gods, Sleipnir of steeds, Bifrost of bridges, Bragi of skalds, Habrok of hawks and Garm of hounds.

(Grimnir reveals himself as Odin.)

45. (44) Now my face have I shown to the war-God's sons, then shall help awake, and the Gods shall gather, all glad, to the bench in Aegir's feasting hall.

46. (50) Dulled with ale are you, Geirrod, too much have you drunk, of great treasure are you deprived, bereaved of my help, and of all chosen warriors, even the favor of Odin.

47. (51) Much have I told you, but little you mind, by tricks you have been betrayed: before long shall I see your sword, good friend, lying all bathed in blood.

48. (52) Your days are run out, the Dread War-father owns him who is slain by the sword: the spirits are hostile, behold now! it is Odin; more near shall you come if you can.

(He makes known his names.)

49. They have called me Hood-winker, called me Wanderer, Helm-bearer, Lord of the Host, Well-comer, Third Highest, Wave, and Slender, High One, Dazzler of Hel.

50. They have called me Soothsayer, True and Fickle, On-driver, Eager in War, Flashing-eyed, Flaming-eyed, Bale-worker, Shape-shifter, Veiled One, Masked One, Wile-wise and Much-wise, Broad-hat, Long-beard, War-father, On-thruster, All-father, Death father, On-rider, Freight-wafter— never was I called by one name alone since I passed through the people of men.

51. They called me Grimnir, the Masked one, at Geirrod's, Jalk was I named at Osmund's, Keeler once, when I drew the sledge, Thror in council, in strife the Stormer, Wish-giver, Wind-roar, Tree-rocker, Equal-ranked, Grey-beard and Wizard of Gods.

THE FORMING VERSES

52. They called me Sage and Wise when I duped the old Jötun who dwells beneath the earth, and slew single-handed the glorious son of that monster who owned the Mead.
53. They call me now Odin, but before that the Dread One, Thund was I called before that, Watcher and Shaker, Wafter and Counselor, Maker and Jalk among Gods, Weaver and Soother, names which I deem come all from Myself alone.

King Geirrod was sitting by with a half-drawn sword across his knees. When he knew that Odin was there, he rose up desiring to remove the God from the fire. But as he did so the sword slipped out of his hand point upwards, while losing his feet he fell forward upon it, and was pierced through and slain. Then Odin vanished, and Agnar was left to rule a long time as king.

NOTES

2. —Rule the realm or land of the Goths, a name used in a general sense for warriors or a nation.
5. —Frey, Elf-home, see [Bray's] Intro. to Skm. and Ls. st. 43. Tooth-gift; gift to a child at teething.
7. —"Falling-brook": Sokkvabekkr has usually been rendered Sinking-bench; Detter suggests the above.
8. Odin, here called Hropt: See [Bray's] Intro.
11.. —Thiazi, Skadi, see Ls. st. 50 and Introd. Jötun or giant; J in Icelandic is pronounced like Y; so also Freyja, Njord.
14. —Freyja seems here to stand for Frigg, wife of Odin, who shared the slain with him.
16. —Njord in that haven; the suggested meaning for Noatun is "Ship-haven," see Frag. from Sn.E, and Saga-book, v., 797, 192.
17. —Vidar, see Vm. st. 53: Vsp. st. 54.
18.—Thunder-flood. The river name Thund may so be connected with Icl. Thunor by the suffix th (V), or, meaning Swollen, with Icl. pindan (B). The fish of the mighty Wolf is according to G. the sun, or prey of the wolf of darkness, st. 39:

she shines in the heavens till swallowed by Fenrir; see Vm. 46. Cf. Dt. HI. who translate the Wolfs flood or stream which flowed from his jaws, and connect the passage with the storming of Asgard by the Wanes mentioned in Vsp. 24.

21. —See Vsp. st. 43.

23., 24.—Wolves, ravens: these particulars are taken from Sn.E., who had evidently other sources than Grm. for his description.

27., 28. [Deleted] —The names contained in these strophes do not all bear interpretation and seem to belong to existing, not mythical, rivers, some of which were to be found in Britain.

31. —Yggdrasil's ash, the World Tree; see Vsp. st. 2, 19; Hav. st.

35. —Fierce-stinger, dragon of the underworld; set Vsp. st.39.

37. Human kind. —These are the dead Folk whose dwelling is in the underworld (see Vsp. st. 52), not, as Snorri suggests, the living. We are repeatedly told that Yggdrasil springs from under the earth. (Dt. HI.) Hel, see Bdr. st. 1.

36. —Valkyries, or war maidens of Odin; see Vsp. st. 31.

39. Skoll, Moon-hater, wolves of darkness; see Vsp. st. 40. Fenrir, the great Wolf who swallows Odin; see Vsp. st. 53.

40. —Ymir, a Jötun, the first born of beings; see Vm. st. 21, 29.

41. Middle Earth: In Old English poems also the earth is called Middle-garth.

42. —So understood by the Copenhagen edition (1848). When the kettle is taken off the Gods can see Odin through the roof opening, come to his rescue, and then hold a triumphal feast; see st. 45 (G. J. L.). Dt. HI. explain it in connection with the strophe following. The house was set open to guests at meal-time, and he who so first invited a God and kindled the friendly hearth fire was regarded as one of the benefactors of the Folk.

43. —The Wielder's sons are rival forgers of the Sparkler's kin; see Vsp. st. 37. 44. Skidbladnir, see Saga- book, iv., 192, 193.

45. —Aegir's feasting hall, see Ls.

51.—Tree-rocker, Odin as Wind God. Another meaning suggested for Biflindi is Shield-shaker.

52. —The old Jötun, Suttung, who owned the Song-mead; see Hav. st. 10

THE WISDOM OF ALL-WISE
[The Dwarf]

All-wise.
1. Before long shall a bride deck the bench beside me, we will hurry home together: swift in my wooing shall I seem to all beings, but at home none shall hinder my peace.
Thor.
2. What being are you so pale of hue? Have you dwelled to-night with the dead? A likeness to giants I believe hangs over you; you were not born for a bride!
All-wise.
3. I am All-wise who dwells far under the Earth, I hide in a rock for my home; I look for the Thunderer, Lord of the goat-wain: let none break a firm-sworn vow.
Thor.
4. I will break it, who rule over the bride as father; he alone among Gods is the giver: I was far from home when that fair maid of mine was promised you ever as bride.
All-wise.
5. What hero is this, who holds in his power that fair glowing maiden as gift? Like a far-straying arrow, none knows who you are, nor from where all the wealth which you wear.
Thor.
6. Winged-thunder am I, wide have I wandered, son of Sigrani Long-bearded: never with my will shall you win the young maiden and get you a wife among Gods.
All-wise.
7. Your good-will then must I speedily gain and win me a wife among Gods: I would readily hold in my arms than lack that snow-white maiden as mine.
Thor.
8. The maiden's love you shall not lack, stranger, who seems wise! if you can tell out of every world all that I long to learn.
9. Tell me this, All-wise, since you are learned in the ways of all beings, I see: —how is Earth, which lies spread before sons of men, named by the beings of all worlds.

All-wise.
10. Earth it is named among men, but Field among Gods, Wanes call it ever the Way; Jötuns, Fair Green, Elves, the Grower, High Powers call it Clay.

Thor.
11. Tell me this, All-wise, since you are learned in the ways of all beings I see: —how is Heaven, which once was born of Ymir named by the beings of all worlds?

All-wise.
12. Heaven it is named among men, Time-teller among Gods, Wanes call it Weaver of Wind, Jötuns, Overworld, Elves, the Fair Roof, dwarfs, the Dripping Hall.

Thor.
13. Tell me this, All-wise, since you are learned in the ways of all beings, I see: —how is the Moon which men behold named by the beings of all worlds?

All-wise.
14. Moon it is named among men, the Ball among Gods, but the Whirling Wheel in Hel, of Jötuns, the Hastener, of dwarfs, the Shimmerer, it is Year-teller called of Elves.

Thor.
15. Tell me this, All-wise, since you are learned in the ways of all beings, I see: —how is Sol which the sons of men behold named by the beings of all worlds?

All-wise.
16. Sol it is named among men, but Sun among Gods, dwarfs call it Dallier's playmate, Ever-glowing, the Jötuns, Fair wheel, the Elves, All-shine, the children of Gods.

Thor.
17. Tell me this, All-wise, since you are learned in the ways of all beings, I see: —how are Clouds of the sky, that with showers are mingled, named by the beings of all worlds?

All-wise.
18. They are clouds among men, Shower-promise to Gods, Wind-floater called of Wanes, Rain-omen of Jötuns, Storm-might of Elves, Helm of the Hidden in Hel.

THE FORMING VERSES

Thor.
19. Tell me this, All-wise, since you are learned in the ways of all beings, I see: —how is the Wind which wanders wide named by the beings of all worlds?

All-wise.
20. Wind it is named among men, but Waverer of Gods, the wise Powers call it Whinnier, Jötuns, the Howler, Elves, Roaring Rider, in Hel it is called Swooping Storm.

Thor.
21. Tell me this, All-wise, since you are learned in the ways of all beings, I see: —how is the Calm, ever wanting to rest, named by the beings of all worlds?

All-wise.
22. Calm it is named among men, Sea-rest among Gods, Wanes ever call it Wind-lull, Jötuns, the Swelterer, Elves, Day-soother, dwarfs, the Refuge of Day.

Thor.
23. Tell me this, All-wise, since you are learned in the ways of all beings, I see: —how is the Sea which is sailed of men, named by the beings of all worlds?

All-wise.
24. Sea it is named among men, Wide Ocean of Gods, Wanes call it flowing Wave, Jötuns, Eel-home, Elves, the Water-stave, by dwarfs it is called the Deep.

Thor.
25. Tell me this, All-wise, since you are learned in the ways of all beings, I see: how is Fire, which burns before men's sons, named by the beings of all worlds?

All-wise.
26. Fire it is named among men, but Flame among Gods, Wanes call it leaping Wave, Jötuns, the Ravener, Hel-Folk, the Racer, dwarfs, the Burning Bane.

Thor.
27. Tell me this, All-wise, since you are learned in the ways of all beings, I see: how is Wood which waxes before men's sons named by the beings of all worlds?

All-wise.
28. Wood it is named among men, Wold-locks among Gods, by heroes Sea-weed of the hills, Jötuns, Life-feeder, Elves, the Fair-limbed, Waves ever call it Wand.
Thor.
29. Tell me this, All-wise, since you are learned in the ways of all beings, I see: how is Night who is born, the daughter of Norr, named by the beings of all worlds?
All-wise.
30. She is Night among men, but Mist among Gods, the High Powers call her Hood, the Jötuns, Unlight, Elves, the Sleep-joy, dwarfs, the Goddess of Dreams.
Thor.
31. Tell me this, All-wise, since you are learned in the ways of all beings, I see: —how is Seed which is sown by the sons of men named by the beings of all worlds?
All-wise.
32. It is named Barley among men, but Bear among Gods, Wanes call it Growth of the ground, Jötuns, Food-stuff, Elves, the Sap-staff, Hel-dwellers, Drooping Head.
Thor.
33. Tell me this, All-wise, since you are learned in the ways of all beings, I see: —how is Ale which sons of men drink often named by the beings of all worlds?
All-wise.
34. Ale it is named among men, but Beer among Gods, the Stirring Drink of Wanes, of Jötuns, Clear-flowing, of Hel-Folk, Mead, by the Sons of Suttung, Feast.
Thor.
35. Not ever have I found in the bosom of one more learning of olden lore; but with tricks are you duped, so dallying here, while dawn is upon you, dwarf! Behold! Sun shines in the hall.
(All-wise the dwarf is turned into stone.)

THE FORMING VERSES

NOTES

3. —The goat-wain, Thor's chariot; see Hym. st. 7, 38, see [Bray's] Introd. thrk.

6. —Sigrani, a name for Odin in his form of an old man with a long beard.

11. —Born of Ymir, see Grm. st. 40; Vm. st. 21 and [Bray's] Introd.

14. —Ball, a doubtful word. G. V. suggest Fire. Hastener, because pursued by a wolf; see Grm. st. 39.

16. —Dallier's playmate. The sun makes sport of dwarfs who are caught above ground at dawn; st. 35.

20. —Waverer, one of Odin's names as Wind-God.

24. —Wide Ocean, others suggest Silent Water.

28. —Heroes, the dead warriors in Hel, Icelandic halir, is used elsewhere for the dead (See Vm. st. 43) and has probably the same meaning here.

32. Bear is an old word for barley, and cognate with the Icelandic barr.

THE WORDS OF THE MIGHTY WEAVER

Odin.
1. Now counsel me, Frigg for I gladly would seek the Mighty Weaver of words. I yearn to strive with that all-wise giant in learning of olden lore.
Frigg.
2. Rather, Father of Hosts! I gladly would keep you at home in the garden of the Gods; no giant I deem so dread and wise as that Mighty Weaver of words.
Odin.
3. Far have I fared much have I ventured, often have I proved the Powers; this now must I know how the house-folk fare in the Mighty Weaver's home.
4. Then safely go, come safely again, and safely travel your way: may your wit avail you, Father of beings, when you weave words with the giant!
5. Then Odin went to prove with words the wisdom of the all-wise giant: he reached the hall of the Jötun Folk; the Dread One entered forthwith.
Odin.
6. Hail, Mighty Weaver! here in this hall I have come yourself to see; and first will try if you are in truth all-wise and all-knowing, Giant.
Weaver.
7. What man is here, who dares in my hall to throw his words at me so? you shall never come forth again from our courts if you be not the wiser of two.
Odin.
8. Riddle-reader I am called, I come from my roaming thirsty here to your halls, in need of welcome and kindly greeting, long way have I wandered, Giant.
Weaver.
9. Why speak, Riddle-reader, standing so? take here your seat in the hall; and soon shall be seen who knows the more, stranger or ancient sage.

THE FORMING VERSES

Odin.
10. Let the penniless wretch in the house of the rich speak needful words or none: babbling, I see, works ill for him who comes to the cold in heart.

I. (The Proving of Riddle-reader.)

Weaver.
11. Say, Riddle-reader! since on the floor you gladly would show your skill, how the Steed is called which draws each Day over the children of men.

Odin.
12. It is Shining-Mane who draws bright Day over the children of men; they hold him best of steeds in the host; streams light from his mane evermore.

Weaver.
13. Say, Riddle-reader! since on the floor you gladly would show your skill, how the Steed is called who forth from the east draws Night over the blessed Powers.

Odin.
14. It is Frosty-Mane who draws evermore each Night over the blessed Powers; he lets fall drops from his bit each dawning; then comes dew in the valleys.

Weaver.
15. Say, Riddle-reader! since on the floor you gladly would show your skill, how the River is called which parts the realm of the Jötun Folk from the Gods.

Odin.
16. That River is Ifing which parts the realm of the Jötun Folk from the Gods; free shall it flow while life's days last; never ice shall come over that stream.

Weaver.
17. Say, Riddle-reader! since on the floor you gladly would show your skill, how the Field is called where in strife shall meet dark Surt and the gracious Gods.

Odin.
18. War-path is the Field where in strife shall meet dark Surt and the gracious Gods: a hundred miles it measures each way; it is the Field marked out by Fate.

Weaver.
19. Wise are you, stranger, but come now and sit by my side on the Jötun's seat; let us talk and wager on wisdom of mind our two heads here in the hall.
(Odin seats himself by the giant.)

II. (The Proving of the Mighty Weaver.)

Odin.
20. Answer well the first, if you have the wit, and know, Mighty Weaver, from where the Earth and the heavens on high, wise Giant, came once to be.
Weaver.
21. From the flesh of Ymir the world was formed, from his bones were mountains made, and Heaven from the skull of that frost-cold giant, from his blood the billows of the sea.
Odin.
22. Answer well the second, if you have the wit, and know, Mighty Weaver, —when Moon has come who fares over men, and when Sun has had her source.
Weaver.
23. The Mover of the Handle is father of Moon, and the father also of Sun, round the heavens they roll each day for measuring of years to men.
Odin.
24. Answer well the third if you have the wit, and know, Mighty Weaver, when Day arose to pass over the Folk, and Night with her waning Moons.
Weaver.
25. There is one called Dawning, the father of Day, but Night was born of Norr; new and waning moons the wise Powers wrought for measuring of years to men.
Odin.
26. Answer well the fourth, if you have the wit, and know, Mighty Weaver, —when Winter came and warm Summer first the wise Powers once among.

THE FORMING VERSES

Weaver.
27. There is One called Sweetsouth, father of Summer, but Wind-cool is winter's sire, the son was he of Sorrow-seed; all fierce and dread is that Folk.

Odin.
28. Answer well the fifth, if you have the wit, and know, Mighty Weaver: —who was born of Gods or of Jötun brood, the eldest in days of old?

Weaver.
29. Untold winters before Earth was fashioned roaring Bergelm was born; his father was Thrudgelm of Mighty Voice, loud-sounding Ymir his grandsire.

Odin.
30. Answer well the sixth, if you have the wit, and know, Mighty Weaver, —when came Ymir, loud-sounding Jötun, the first of your generation, wise Giant.

Weaver.
31. From Stormy-billow sprang poison-drops, which grew into Jötun form, and from him are come the whole of our kin; all fierce and dread is that Folk.

Odin.
32. Answer well the seventh, if you have the wit, and know, Mighty Weaver, —how that ancient Being begot his children who knew not joy of a giantess.

Weaver.
33. It is said that under the Frost-giant's arm grew a boy and girl together; foot with foot begot of that first wise giant, and a six-headed son was born.

Odin.
34. Answer well the eighth, if you have the wit, and know, Mighty Weaver, —what mind you of old, and did earliest know? since I see you are all wise, giant!

Weaver.
35. Untold winters before Earth was shaped, roaring Bergelm was born; I mind me first when that most wise giant of old in a mill-cradle was laid.

Odin.
36. Answer well the ninth, if you have the wit, and know, Mighty Weaver, —when comes the Wind which fares over the waves, but which never man has seen.

Weaver.
37. Corpse-swallower sits at the end of heaven, a Jötun in eagle form; from his wings, they say, comes the wind which fares over all the dwellers of Earth.

Odin.
38. Answer well the tenth, since all tidings of Gods you know, Mighty Weaver, —where Njord first came amid the Aesir kin —courts and altars he owns in hundreds —who was not reared in their Folk.

Weaver.
39. In Wane-home once the wise Powers made him and gave him as hostage to Gods; in the story of time he shall yet come home to the wise foreseeing Wanes.

Odin.
40. Answer well the eleventh, since they call you wise, if you know, Mighty Weaver —who are the beings who so do battle in the dwellings of Odin each day?

Weaver.
41. All the Chosen Warriors are waging war in the dwellings of Odin each day: they choose the slain, ride home from the strife, then at peace sit again together.

Odin.
42. Answer well the twelfth, how all the story of the Powers you know, Weaver. —Can you truly tell me the secrets of Jötuns and all the Gods, wise giant?

Weaver.
43. Most truly I can tell you the secrets of Jötuns and all the Gods; since I have been into every world, even nine worlds to Mist-Hel beneath where die the dead from Hel.

Odin.
44. Far have I fared, much have I ventured, often have I proved the Powers: what beings shall live when the long Dread Winter comes over the people of earth?

THE FORMING VERSES

Weaver.
45. Life and Life-craver, who hidden shall lie in the boughs of Yggdrasil's Ash: morning dews they shall have as meat; then shall come new kindred's of men.

Odin.
46. Far have I fared, much have I ventured, often have I proved the Powers: when comes a new Sun in the clear heaven again when the Wolf has swallowed the old.

Weaver.
47. One daughter alone shall that Elf-beam bear before she is swallowed by the Wolf; and the maid shall ride on the mother's path after the Powers have perished.

Odin.
48. Far have I fared, much have I ventured, often have I proved the Powers: who are those maidens who pass over the sea wandering, wise in mind?

Weaver.
49. There fly three troops of Mogthrasir's maidens and hover over homes of men; the only guardian spirits on earth, and they are of Jötuns born.

Odin.
50. Far have I fared, much have I ventured, often have I proved the Powers: who shall afterwards hold the wealth of the Gods when the fire of dark Surt is slaked?

Weaver.
51. In the places of the Gods shall dwell Vidar and Vali when the fire of dark Surt is slaked; to Modi and Magni shall Mjöllnir be given when to Thor comes the end of strife.

Odin.
52. Far have I fared, much have I ventured, often have I proved the Powers: what foe shall bring, at the Doom of Gods, to Odin the end of life?

Weaver.
53. Fenrir shall swallow the Father of men, but this shall Vidar avenge: with his sword he shall split the ice-cold jaws of the mighty monster in strife.

Odin.
54. Far have I fared, much have I ventured, often have I proved the Powers: what spoke Odin's self in the ear of his son, when Baldr was laid on the cremation fire?
Weaver.
55. That no man knows, what You did speak of old in the ear of your son. So with fated lips have I uttered old lore and told the great Doom of the Powers; for I have striven in word-skill with Odin's self; you are ever the wisest of all.

NOTES
16. —*Ifing is probably the river mentioned in Hrbl., st. 2.*
17. —*Surt, a fire giant; see st. 50 and Vsp. st. 52, 53, Ls. st. 42.*
21. —*Ymir, the first-born of Jötuns; see st. 29, Grm. st, 40, Vsp. st. 3.*
22. —*Moon, sun, see Grm. st. 31.*
23. —*Mover of the handle. This mysterious being Mundilferi is not mentioned elsewhere. Rydberg traces a belief that the heavens were turned by a gigantic world mill. (Teutonic Mythology, p. 397).*
25. —*Norr, see Alv.st.*
29. —*In this passage Ymir is called Aurgelmir; "gelmir" in all these names seems to signify the roaring, rushing sound of the elemental powers in chaos.*
31. —*Stormy-billow, a mythical river between Asgard and Jötunheim; see Hym. st. 5, Sn.E. c. 5.*
35. —*Cradle. Icelandic lupr has various meanings meal-bin box, boat, ark; see [Bray's] Intro.*
37. —*Corpse-swallower is perhaps identical with the raven of Vsp. 47.*
38, 39. —*Aesir, Wanes. These are the two categories of Gods; for their war, see Vsp. st. 21-24 and [Bray's] Introd. to Vsp.*
41. —*Chosen Warriors, see Grm. st. 21.*
43. —*Nine Worlds. Nine was a mystic number; Hdv. 137, Skm. 21, 39, etc. In Alv. are mentioned worlds of Aesir, Wanes, giants,*

THE FORMING VERSES

dwarfs, Elves, men, and the dead in Hel, but nine are never enumerated; Cf. Vsp. 2.

44. —Dread Winter or Fimbul-vetr is the sign of the coming doom of the Gods (st. 51) mentioned by Snorri; see also Hdl. st. 16.

45. —Yggdrasil is suggested by Hödd-mimir's wood; Cf. Mimameid Fj. st. 14 18, and Introd. Hav., which is clearly the World tree.

46. —The Wolf, Fenrir.

49. —Mogthrasir is unknown. The interpretation "Son-craver" suggested by G. is doubtful.

51. —Vidar, see Grm. 17, Vsp. 54, and Vali, both sons of Odin; see Bdr. st. 11. Modi, see Hym. st. 35, and Magni, see Hrbl. st. 9; both sons of Thor. Mjöllnir, Thor's hammer; see Thrk. and [Bray's] Introd. To Thor comes the end: he is slain by the World-serpent, Vsp. st. 56. He is here called Vingnir; set A lv., st. 6.

54. —See Bdr., st. No. 10.

THE WORDS OF ODIN
THE HIGH ONE

(Wisdom for Wanderers and Counsel to Guests)

1. At every door-way, before one enters, one should spy round, one should pry round, for uncertain is the knowing that there be no foeman sitting within, before one on the floor.

2. Hail, you Givers! a guest is come; say! where shall he sit within? Much pressed is he who gladly on the hearth would seek for warmth and good.

3. He has need of fire, who now is come, numbed with cold to the knees; food and clothing the wanderer craves who has fared over the frosty mountain.

4. He craves for water, who comes for refreshment, drying off and friendly bidding, marks of good will, fair fame if it is won, and welcome once and again.

5. He has need of his wits who wanders wide, anything simple will serve at home; but a gazing-stock is the fool who sits with the wise, and nothing knows.

6. Let no man glory in the greatness of his mind, but rather keep watch over his wits. Cautious and silent let him enter a dwelling; to the heedful comes seldom harm, for none can find a more faithful friend than his wealth of mother wit.

7. Let the wary stranger who seeks refreshment keep silent with sharpened hearing; with his ears let him listen, and look with his eyes; so each wise man spies out the way.

8. Happy is he who wins for himself fair fame and kindly words; but uneasy is that which a man does own while it lies in another's breast.

9. Happy is he who has in himself praise and wisdom in life; for often does a man ill counsel get when it is born in another's breast.

10. A better burden can no man bear on the way than his mother wit: it is the refuge of the poor, and richer it seems than wealth in a world untried.

11. A better burden can no man bear on the way than his mother wit: and no worse provision can he carry with him than too deep a drink of ale.

THE FORMING VERSES

12. Less good than they say for the sons of men is the drinking often of ale: for the more they drink, the less can they think and keep a watch over their wits.

13. A bird of Unmindfulness flutters over ale feasts, wiling away men's wits: with the feathers of that fowl I was fettered once in the gardens of Gunnlod below.

14. Drunk was I then, I was over drunk in that crafty Fjalar's court. But best is an ale feast when man is able to call back his wits at once.

15. Silent and thoughtful and bold in strife the prince's child should be. Joyous and generous let each man show him until he shall suffer death.

16. A coward believes he will ever live if he keep himself safe from strife: but old age leaves him not long in peace though spears may spare his life.

17. A fool will gape when he goes to a friend, and mumble only, or mope; but pass him the ale cup and all in a moment the mind of that man is shown.

18. He knows alone who has wandered wide, and far has fared on the way, what manner of mind a man does own who is wise of head and heart.

19. Keep not the mead cup but drink your measure; speak needful words or none: none shall upbraid you for lack of breeding if soon you seek your rest.

20. A greedy man, if he be not mindful, eats to his own life's hurt: often the belly of the fool will bring him to scorn when he seeks the circle of the wise.

21. Herds know the hour of their going home and turn themselves from the grass; but never is found a foolish man who knows the measure of his mouth.

22. The miserable man and evil minded makes of all things mockery, and knows not that which he best should know, that he is not free from faults.

23. The unwise man is awake all night, and ponders everything over; when morning comes he is weary in mind, and all is a burden as ever.

24. The unwise man sees all who smile and flatter him are his friends, nor notes how often they speak him ill when he sits in the circle of the wise.

25. The unwise man sees all who smile and flatter him are his friends; but when he shall come into court he shall find there are few to defend his cause.

26. The unwise man thinks all to know, while he sits in a sheltered nook; but he knows not one thing, what he shall answer, if men shall put him to proof.

27. For the unwise man it is best to be mute when he comes amid the crowd, for none is aware of his lack of wit if he wastes not too many words; for he who lacks wit shall never learn though his words flow never so fast.

28. Wise he is deemed who can question well, and also answer back: the sons of men can no secret make of the tidings told in their midst.

29. Too many unstable words are spoken by him who never holds his peace; the hasty tongue sings its own mishap if it be not bridled in.

30. Let no man be held as a laughing-stock, though he come as guest for a meal: wise enough seem many while they sit dry-skinned and are not put to proof.

31. A guest thinks him witty who mocks at a guest and runs from his wrath away; but none can be sure who jests at a meal that he makes not fun among foes.

32. Often, though their hearts lean towards one another, friends are divided at table; ever the source of strife it will be, that guest will anger guest.

33. A man should take always his meals early unless he visit a friend, or he sits and mopes, and half famished seems, and can ask or answer nothing.

34. Long is the round to a false friend leading, even if he dwell on the way; but though far off fared, to a faithful friend straight are the roads and short.

35. A guest must depart again on his way, nor stay in the same place ever; if he stay too long on another's bench the loved one soon becomes loathed.

THE FORMING VERSES

36. One's own house is best, though small it may be; each man is master at home; though he have but two goats and a bark-thatched hut, it is better than craving a blessing.

37. One's own house is best, though small it may be, each man is master at home; with a bleeding heart will he beg, who must, his meat at every meal.

38. Let a man never stir on his road a step without his weapons of war; for unsure is the knowing when need shall arise of a spear on the way outside.

39. I found none so noble or free with his food, who was not gladdened with a gift, nor one who gave of his gifts such store but he loved reward, could he win it.

40. Let no man withhold him and suffer need of the wealth he has won in life; often is saved for a foe what was meant for a friend, and much goes worse than one sees.

41. With cloaks and arms shall friends gladden each other, so has one proved oneself; for friends last longest, if fate be fair, who give and give again.

42. To his friend a man should bear him as friend, and gift for gift bestow, laughter for laughter let him exchange, but lying pay for a lie.

43. To his friend a man should bear him as friend, to him and a friend of his; but let him beware that he be not the friend of one who is friend to his foe.

44. Have you a friend whom you trust well, from whom you crave good? Share your mind with him, gifts exchange with him, fare to find him often.

45. But have you one whom you trusted ill yet from whom you crave good? You shall speak him fair, but falsely think, and lying pay for a lie.

46. Yet further of him whom you trusted ill, and whose mind you do doubt; you shall laugh with him but withhold your thought, for gift with like gift should be paid.

47. Young was I once, I walked alone, and bewildered seemed in the way; then I found me another and rich I thought me, for man is the joy of man.

48. Most blessed is he who lives free and bold and nurses never a grief, for the fearful man is dismayed by anything, and the mean one mourns over giving.

49. My garments once I gave in the field to two tree-men made as men; heroes they seemed when once they were clothed; it is the naked who suffer shame!

50. The pine tree wastes which is perched on the hill, not bark nor needles shelter it; such is the man whom none does love; for what should he longer live?

51. Fiercer than fire among ill friends for five days love will burn; but soon it is quenched, when the sixth day comes, and all friendship soon is spoiled.

52. Not great things alone must one give to another, praise often is earned for nothing; with half a loaf and a tilted bowl I have found me many a friend.

53. Little the sand if little the seas, little are minds of men, for never in the world were all equally wise, it is shared by the fools and the sage.

54. Wise in measure let each man be; but let him not grow too wise; for never the happiest of men is he who knows much of many things.

55. Wise in measure should each man be; but let him not grow too wise; seldom a heart will sing with joy if the owner be all too wise.

56. Wise in measure should each man be, but never let him grow too wise: who looks not forward to learn his fate unburdened heart will bear.

57. Torch kindles from torch until it be burned, spark is kindled from spark, man unfolds him by speech with man, but grows over secret through silence.

58. He must rise soon who gladly of another or life or wealth would win; scarce falls the prey to sleeping wolves, or to slumberers victory in strife.

59. He must rise soon who has few to serve him, and see to his work himself; who sleeps at morning is hindered much, to the keen is wealth half-won.

THE FORMING VERSES

60. Of dry logs saved and roof-bark stored a man can know the measure, of fire-wood too which should last him out quarter and half years to come.

61. Fed and washed should one ride to court though in garments none too new; you shall not shame yourself for shoes or pants, nor yet for a lesser steed.

62. Like an eagle swooping over old ocean, snatching after his prey, so comes a man into court who finds there are few to defend his cause.

63. Each man who is wise and would wise be called must ask and answer rightly. Let one know your secret, but never a second, —then three thousand shall know.

64. A wise counseled man will be mild in bearing and use his might in measure, or else when he come his fierce foes among, he find others fiercer than he.

65. Each man should be watchful and wary in speech, and slow to put trust in a friend. For the words which one to another speaks he may win reward of ill.

66. At many a feast I was far too late, and much too soon at some; drunk was the ale or yet unserved: never hits he the meatjoint who is hated.

67. Here and there to a home I had by chance been asked had I needed no meat at my meals, or were two hams left hanging in the house of that friend where I had partaken of one.

68. Most dear is fire to the sons of men, most sweet the sight of the sun; good is health if one can but keep it, and to live a life without shame.

69. Not robbed of all is he who is ill, for some are blessed in their children, some in their kin and some in their wealth, and some in working well.

70. More blessed are the living than the lifeless, it is the living who comes by the cow; I saw the hearth-fire burn in the rich man's hall and himself lying dead at the door.

71. The lame can ride horse, the handless drive cattle, the deaf one can fight and prevail, it is happier for the blind than for him on the bale-fire, for no man has care for a corpse.

72. Best have a son though he be late born and before him the father be dead: seldom are stones on the wayside raised unless by kinsmen to kinsmen.

73. Two are hosts against one, the tongue is the head's curse, beneath a rough hide a hand may be hid; he is glad at nightfall who knows of his lodging, short is the ship's berth, and changeful the autumn night, much veers the wind before the fifth day and blows round yet more in a month.

74. He that learns nothing will never know how one is the fool of another, for if one be rich another is poor and for that should bear no blame.

75. Cattle die and kinsmen die, you yourself too soon must die, but one thing never, I see, will die, —fair fame of one who has earned.

76. Cattle die and kinsmen die, you yourself too soon must die, but one thing never, I see, will die, —the doom on each one dead.

77. Full-stocked folds had the Failing's sons, who bear now a beggar's staff: brief is wealth, as the winking of an eye, most faithless ever of friends.

78. If by chance a fool should find for himself wealth or a woman's love, pride grows in him but wisdom never and onward he fares in his folly.

79. All will prove true that you ask of runes—those that are come from the Gods, which the High Powers wrought, and which Odin painted; then silence is surely best.

(Maxims for All Men.)

80. Praise day at even, a wife when dead, a weapon when tried, a maid when married, ice when it is crossed, and ale when it is drunk.

81. Hew wood in wind, sail the seas in a breeze, woo a maid in the dark, —for day's eyes are many, —work a ship for its gliding, a shield for its shelter, a sword for its striking, a maid for her kiss;

82. Drink ale by the fire, but slide on the ice; buy a steed when it is lanky, a sword when it is rusty; feed your horse beneath a roof, and your hound in the yard.

THE FORMING VERSES

83. The speech of a maiden should no man trust nor the words which a woman says; for their hearts were shaped on a whirling wheel and falsehood fixed in their breasts.

84. Breaking bow, or flaring flame, ravening wolf, or croaking raven, routing swine, or rootless tree, growing wave, or seething cauldron,

85. flying arrows, or falling billow, ice of a night time, coiling snake, woman's bed-talk, or broken blade, play of bears, or a prince's child,

86. sickly calf or self-willed thrall, witches flattery, new-slain foe, brother's slayer, though seen on the highway, half burned house, or horse too swift—useless is it with one leg broken—be never so trustful, as these to trust.

87. Let none put faith in the first sown fruit nor yet in his son too soon; whim rules the child and weather the field, each is open to chance.

88. Like the love of women whose thoughts are lies, is the driving un-roughshod over slippery ice of a two year old, ill-tamed and gay; or in a wild wind steering a helmless ship, or the lame catching reindeer in the frost-thawed fell.

(Lessons for Lovers.)

89. Now plainly I speak, since both I have seen; unfaithful is man to maid; we speak them fairest when thoughts are falsest and wile the wisest of hearts.

90. —Let him speak soft words and offer wealth who longs for a woman's love, praise the shape of the shining maid—he wins who so does woo.

91. —Never a bit should one blame another whom love has brought into bonds: often a witching form will fetch the wise which holds not the heart of fools.

92. Never a bit should one blame another for a folly which many befalls; the might of love makes sons of men into fools who once were wise.

93. The mind knows alone what is nearest the heart and sees where the soul is turned: no sickness seems to the wise so sore as in nothing to know content.

(Odin's Love Quests.)

94. This once I felt when I sat outside in the reeds, and looked for my love; body and soul of me was that sweet maiden yet never I won her as wife.

95. Billing's daughter I found on her bed, fairer than sunlight sleeping, and the sweets of lordship seemed to me nothing but that I lived with that lovely form.

96. 'Yet nearer evening come you, Odin, if you will woo a maiden: all were undone except two knew alone such a secret deed of shame.'

97. So away I turned from my wise intent, and deemed my joy assured, for all her liking and all her love I see that I yet should win.

98. When I came before long the war troop bold were watching and waking all: with burning branches and torches carried they showed me my sorrowful way.

99. Yet nearer morning I went, once more, —the house-folk slept in the hall, but soon I found a barking dog tied fast to that fair maid's couch.

100. Many a sweet maid when one knows her mind is fickle found towards men: I proved it well when that prudent lass I sought to lead astray: shrewd maid, she sought me with every insult and I won then no wife.

(Odin's Quest after the Song Mead.)

101. In your home be joyous and generous to guests, discreet shall you be in your bearing, mindful and talkative, would you gain wisdom, often making mention of good. He is 'Simpleton' named who has nothing to say, for such is the fashion of fools.

102. I sought that old Jötun, now safe am I back, little served my silence there; but whispering many soft speeches I won my desire in Suttung's halls.

103. I bored me a road there with Rati's tusk and made room to pass through the rock; while the ways of the Jötuns stretched over and under I dared my life for a drink.

104. It was Gunnlod who gave me on a golden throne a drink of the glorious mead, but with poor reward did I pay her back for her true and troubled heart.

105. In a wily disguise I worked my will; little is lacking to the wise, for the Soul-stirrer now, sweet Mead of Song, is brought to men's earthly abode.

106. I doubt me if ever again I had come from the realms of the Jötun Folk, had I not served me of Gunnlod, sweet woman, her whom I held in my arms.

107. Came forth, next day, the dread Frost Giants, and entered the High One's hall: they asked—was the Baleworker back amid the Powers, or had Suttung slain him below?

108. A ring-oath Odin I believe had taken—how shall one trust his pledge of loyalty? It was he who stole the mead from Suttung, and Gunnlod caused to weep.

(The Counselling of the Stray-Singer.)

109. It is time to speak from the Sage's Seat; hard by the Well of Wyrd I saw and was silent, I saw and pondered, I listened to the speech of men.

110. Of runes they spoke, and the reading of runes was little withheld from their lips: at the High One's hall, in the High One's hall, I so heard the High One say:—

111. I counsel you, Stray-Singer, accept my counsels, they will be your help if you obey them, they will work your good if you win them: rise never at night time except you are spying or seek a spot outside.

112. I counsel you, Stray-Singer, accept my counsels, they will be your help if you obey them, they will work your good if you win them: you shall never sleep in the arms of a sorceress, lest she should lock your limbs;

113. So shall she charm that you shall not heed the council or words of the king, nor care for your food or the joys of mankind, but fall into sorrowful sleep.

114. I counsel you, Stray-Singer, accept my counsels, they will be your help if you obey them, they will work your good if you win them: seek not ever to draw to yourself in love-whispering another's wife.

115. I counsel you, Stray-Singer, accept my counsels, they will be your help if you obey them, they will work your good if you win them: should you long to fare over mountain and fjord provide you well with food.

116. I counsel you, Stray-Singer, accept my counsels, they will be your help if you obey them, they will work your good if you win them: tell not ever an evil man if misfortunes you befall, from such ill friend you need never seek return for your trustful mind.

117. Wounded to death, have I seen a man by the words of an evil woman; a lying tongue had robbed him of life, and all without reason of right.

118. I counsel you, Stray-Singer, accept my counsels, they will be your help if you obey them, they will work your good if you win them: have you a friend whom you trust well, fare you to find him often; for with brushwood grows and with grasses high the path where no foot does pass.

119. I counsel you, Stray-Singer, accept my counsels, they will be your help if you obey them, they will work your good if you win them: in sweet converse call the righteous to your side, learn a healing song while you live.

120. I counsel you, Stray-Singer, accept my counsels, they will be your help if you obey them, they will work your good if you win them: be never the first with friend of yours to break the bond of fellowship; care shall gnaw your heart if you can not tell all your mind to another.

121. I counsel you, Stray-Singer, accept my counsels, they will be your help if you obey them, they will work your good if you win them: never in speech with a foolish deceiver should you waste a single word.

122. From the lips of such you need not look for reward of yours own good will; but a righteous man by praise will render you firm in favor and love.

123. There is mingling in friendship when man can utter all his whole mind to another; there is nothing so vile as a fickle tongue; no friend is he who but flatters.

124. I counsel you, Stray-Singer, accept my counsels, they will be your help if you obey them, they will work your good if you

THE FORMING VERSES

win them: strive not in three words with a man worse than you; often the worst lays the best one low.

125. I counsel you, Stray-Singer, accept my counsels, they will be your help if you obey them, they will work your good if you win them: be not a shoemaker nor yet a shaft maker save for yourself alone: let the shoe be misshapen, or crooked the shaft, and a curse on your head will be called.

126. I counsel you, Stray-Singer, accept my counsels, they will be your help if you obey them, they will work your good if you win them: when in peril you see you, admit you in peril, nor ever give peace to your foes.

127. I counsel you, Stray-Singer, accept my counsels, they will be your help if you obey them, they will work your good if you win them: rejoice not ever at tidings of ill, but glad let your soul be in good.

128. I counsel you, Stray-Singer, accept my counsels, they will be your help if you obey them: they will work your good if you win them: look not up in battle when men are as beasts, lest the beings bewitch you with spells.

129. I counsel you, Stray-Singer, accept my counsels, they will be your help if you obey them, they will work your good if you win them: would you win joy of a gentle maiden, and lure to whispering of love, you shall make fair promise, and let it be fast, —none will scorn their good who can win it.

130. I counsel you, Stray-Singer, accept my counsels, they will be your help if you obey them, they will work your good if you win them: I pray you be wary, yet not too wary, be wariest of all with ale, with another's wife, and a third thing more, that deceivers outwit you never.

131. I counsel you, Stray-Singer, accept my counsels, they will be your help if you obey them, they will work your good if you win them: hold not in scorn, nor mock in your halls a guest or wandering soul.

132. They know but unsurely who sit within what manner of man is come: none is found so good but some fault attends him, or so ill but he serves for something.

133. I counsel you, Stray-Singer, accept my counsels, they will be your help if you obey them, they will work your good if you

win them: hold never in scorn the old singer; often the counsel of the old is good; come words of wisdom from the withered lips of him left to hang among hides, to rock with the rennet's and swing with the skins.

134. I counsel you, Stray-Singer, accept my counsels, they will be your help if you obey them, they will work your good if you win them: growl not at guests nor drive them from the gate but show yourself gentle to the poor.

135. Mighty is the bar to be moved away for the entering in of all. Shower your wealth, or men shall wish you every ill in your limbs.

136. I counsel you, Stray-Singer, accept my counsels, they will be your help if you obey them, they will work your good if you win them: when ale you drink call upon earth's might—it is earth drinks in the floods. (Earth prevails over drink, but fire over sickness, the oak over binding, the ear corn over witchcraft, the rye spur over rupture, the moon over rages, herb over cattle plagues, runes over harm.)

(Odin's Quest after the Runes.)

137. I believe I hung on that windy Tree nine whole days and nights, stabbed with a spear, offered to Odin, myself to my own self given, high on that Tree of which none has heard from what roots it rises to heaven.

138. None refreshed me ever with food or drink, I peered right down in the deep; crying aloud I lifted the Runes, then back I fell from them.

139. Nine mighty songs I learned from the great son of Bale-thorn, Bestla's sire; I drank a measure of the wondrous Mead, with the Soulstirrer's drops I was showered.

140. Before long I bare fruit, and blossomed full well, I grew and increased in wisdom; word following word, I found me words, deed following deed, I wrought deeds.

141. Hidden Runes shall you seek and interpreted signs, many symbols of might and power, by the great Singer painted, by the High Powers fashioned, carved by the Utterer of Gods.

THE FORMING VERSES

142. For Gods carved Odin, for Elves carved Dain, Dvalin the Dallier for dwarfs, All-wise for Jötuns, and I, of myself, carved some for the sons of men.

143. Do you know how to write, do you know how to read, do you know how to paint, do you know how to prove, do you know how to ask, do you know how to offer, do you know how to send, do you know how to spend?

144. Better ask for too little than offer too much, like the gift should be the benefit; better not to send than to overspend. ...So Odin carved before the world began; Then he rose from the deep, and came again.

(The Song of Spells.)

145. Those songs I know, which not sons of men nor queen in a king's court knows; the first is Help which will bring you help in all woes and in sorrow and strife.

146. A second I know, which the son of men must sing, who would heal the sick.

147. A third I know: if sore need should come of a spell to stay my foes; when I sing that song, which shall blunt their swords, not their weapons nor staves can wound.

148. A fourth I know: if men make fast in chains the joints of my limbs, when I sing that song which shall set me free, spring the fetters from hands and feet.

149. A fifth I know: when I see, by foes shot, speeding a shaft through the host, flies it never so strongly I still can halt it, if I get but a glimpse of its flight.

150. A sixth I know: when some lord would harm me in runes on a moist tree's root, on his head alone shall light the ills of the curse that he called upon mine.

151. A seventh I know: if I see a hall high over the bench-mates blazing, flame it never so fiercely I still can save it, —I know how to sing that song.

152. An eighth I know: which all can sing for their good if they learn it well; where hate shall grow amid the warrior sons, I can calm it soon with that song.

153. A ninth I know: when need befalls me to save my vessel afloat, I hush the wind on the stormy wave, and soothe all the sea to rest.

154. A tenth I know: when at night the witches ride and sport in the air, such spells I weave that they wander home out of skins and wits bewildered.

155. An eleventh I know: if by chance I lead my old comrades out to war, I sing beneath the shields, and they fare forth mightily safe into battle, safe out of battle, and safe return from the strife.

156. A twelfth I know: if I see in a tree a corpse from a noose hanging, such spells I write, and paint in runes, that the being descends and speaks.

157. A thirteenth I know: if the new-born son of a warrior I sprinkle with water, that youth will not fail when he fares to war, never slain shall he bow before sword.

158. A fourteenth I know: if I of necessity must number the Powers to the people of men, I know all the nature of Gods and of Elves which none can know untaught.

159. A fifteenth I know, which Folk-stirrer sang, the dwarf, at the gates of Dawn; he sang strength to the Gods, and skill to the Elves, and wisdom to Odin who utters.

160. A sixteenth I know: when all sweetness and love I would win from some artful wench, her heart I turn, and the whole mind change of that fair-armed lady I love.

161. A seventeenth I know: so that even the shy maiden is slow to shun my love.

162. These songs, Stray-Singer, which man's son knows not, long shall you lack in life, though your good if you win them, your benefit if you obey them, if by chance you gain them.

163. An eighteenth I know: which I never shall tell to maiden or wife of man, except alone to my sister, or by chance to her who folds me fast in her arms; most safe are secrets known to but one—the songs are sung to an end.

164. Now the sayings of the High One are uttered in the hall for the good of men, for the woe of Jötuns, Hail, you who has spoken! Hail, you that know! Hail, you that have hearkened! Use, you who has learned!

THE FORMING VERSES

NOTES

The High One, a name for Odin; see Grm. st. 49.

13. —*Gunnlod; st. 104.*

14. —*That crafty Jötun, Suttung; st. 102. The name Fjalar in the text also belongs to Thor's famous opponent; see Hrbl. st. 26. Possibly it is here used in a general sense for any Jötun.*

49. —*Two land-marks, Vigfusson explains two tree-men.*

50. —*On the hill or in the open. Icelandic þorp has this meaning, beside the more common one of hamlet; G. The context makes it quite clear that an unsheltered spot is intended, but as the Norwegian pine flourishes on the hill and dies out among houses, we may perhaps infer that the poem did not originate in Norway.*

51. —*Five days, the old week before the Christian week of seven days.*

53. —*Many useless suggestions have been made to explain this strophe which is perhaps only a general reflection on the vanity of human nature.*

62. —*The meaning of this strophe is somewhat obscure, but perhaps the idea is that the eagle, wanting to seek his food in the quiet mountain pools, is baffled in face of the stormy sea; see Vsp. 59.*

66. —*Hits the joint; or, as we would say, hits the nail on the head.*

72. —*Stones, Icelandic bautarsteinar were monumental stones set upon the high road, many thousands of which are preserved, some with runic inscriptions.*

73. —*This agrees with the Icelandic proverb: A man's hand may often be found beneath a wolf-skin; but others understand: There is the chance of a fist from under a cloak.*

79. —*Runes, st. 139, 141.*

89. —*Odin has had many love adventures in disguise; see Hrbl. st. 16, 18 30.*

95. —*Billing, a dwarf*

102. —*Suttung, a giant of the underworld, For Snorri's version of this story, see [Bray's] Intro. and cf. Grm. st. 52.*

103. —*Rati or the Gnawer, a tool.*

105. —*The Soul-stirrer*, st. 139. One of Odin's characters is that of Song-giver to man; see st. 141, 759, [Bray's] Intro. and Hdl. st. 3.

107. —*Baleworker*, the name which Odin had given himself in disguise.

108. —*Stray-Singer*, the meaning of Loddfafnir is not yet fully decided; see [Bray's] Intro.

109. —*Well of Wyrd*, the most sacred spot in the world, where the Gods meet in council under Yggdrasil; see Grm. st. 30, Vsp. st. 19.

133. —*Rennets*, in Iceland the maw rennets of a calf were, and are still hung up to dry, and used for curdling milk.

136. —Deals with magic, and belongs to the spell songs rather than here.

137. —*A windy Tree*, this must be Yggdrasil. The same words are used with regard to it under the name of Mimir's tree; see Fj. st. 14.

138. —*Back I fell*, the attainment of the runes had released him from the tree.

139. —*Mimir*, who was a Jötun and Odin's teacher, is presumably the son of the giant Bale-thorn, the grandfather of Odin (Rydberg), although his name is not given here.

142. —*All-wise*, this giant is unknown, unless identical with Much-wise; see Fj.

144. —*Odin*, here called by his name Thund, the meaning of which is unknown; see Grm. st. 53.

154. —*The witches*, or "hedge-riders" who could change their shapes or skins (Icel. hama), were so deprived of their magic powers.

156.— Cf.Bdr.st.3.

157. —*Sprinkle with water*, an old Heathen rite of purification; see rth. st. 6.

159. —*Folk-stirrer*, this dwarf is not mentioned elsewhere.

THE LAY OF HYMIR

1. Of old when the war-Gods their prey had won them, in mood for feasting, and still unsatisfied, they shook divining twigs, scanned the blood drops, and found all dainties in Aegir's halls.

2. As the rock-giant sat in his wave-brood rejoicing, and seemed in likeness the son of Mist-blind, came Thor and looked in his eyes with threatening: 'Make now a goodly feast for the Gods!'

3. But the harsh-voiced hero angered the giant, who directly pondered revenge on the Powers; He asked the Thunderer bring him a cauldron 'Wherein for all of you ale I may brew;'

4. The glorious Gods, the Holy Powers such vessel as this could nowhere find; till Tyr the trusty whispered in secret words of friendly counsel to Thor.

Tyr.

5. 'There dwells to the east of Stormy Billow the all-wise Hymir, at heaven's end, my fierce-souled father, who owns the kettle, the broad-roomed cauldron, a full mile deep.'

Thor.

6. 'Do you know can we win that water-seether?'

Tyr.

'If we use our wits, my friend!'

7. So forth they drove through the live-long day till they came from Asgard to Egil's home. He stalled the goats of the splendid horns, while they turned to the hall which Hymir owned.

8. Unsightly seemed to Tyr his granddam, for heads she had nine hundred in all; but another came all golden forth, fair-browed, and bearing to her son the ale-cup.

Hymir's wife.

9. 'Kinsman of giants! gladly would I hide you beneath those cauldrons, though bold of heart; for my lord and master oftentimes shows him mean to strangers, moved soon to wrath.'

10. Long tarried that monster, fierce-mooded Hymir, before he came from his hunting home. He entered the hall, and icicles clashed —all frozen was the bushy beard on his chin.
Wife.
11. 'Hail to you, Hymir! Be gracious in mood: for here in your halls is come our offspring whom long we awaited from distant ways; and with him fares the foe of giants, the friend of man, whose name is Warder.'

12. 'Do you see where they hide, the hall-gable under, sheltering themselves with a pillar between?' But the column was shattered at the glance of the giant, the mighty rafter was torn apart:

13. Down from the beam eight cauldrons crashed, one, hard-hammered, alone was whole. Then forth they stepped, but the ancient Jötun ever followed the foe with his eyes.

14. For evil whispered his mind when he saw the curse of giant-wives stand on the hearth; yet took they soon of the oxen three, and Hymir bade them cook forthwith.

15. Each one left they less by a head, and laid them soon on the seething fire; then before he slumbered the Thunderer ate, himself alone, of the oxen, two.

16. But Hymir the old friend of Hrungnir deemed too ample the meal of Thor: 'Tomorrow at eve shall we three have nothing save our hunting spoil whereon to sup.'

17. Spoke Thor, and said he would fish in the sea, if the fierce-souled giant would find him bait.
Hymir.
18. 'Go, if you dare, slayer of rock-giants, seek your bait from the herd yourself: for such as you I see it will seem that bait from an ox were easy to win.'

19. Directly sped Thor, and soon, all dark, then over its horns struck, and sundered bold youth, to the wood stood an ox before him; the slayer of Jötuns the head, high-towering.
Hymir.
20. 'It seems you are worse by far on foot than at table sitting, Steerer of boats!'

THE FORMING VERSES

21. Then the Lord of goats, told the low-born churl drive the launched sea-horse further from shore; but little he wished, that wary giant, to row any further over the ocean.
22. Alone the famous and fierce-souled Hymir caught on his hook two whales at once; but back in the stern the son of Odin fashioned with craft his fishing line.
23. Lone Serpent-slayer, and Shield of Men, he baited his hook with the head of the ox, and he whom the Gods hate stared there at, the Girdle lying all lands beneath.
24. Then Thor drew mightily—swift in his doing—the poison-glistening snake to the side. His hammer he lifted and struck from on high the fearful head of Fenrir's brother.
25. Moaned the wild monster, the rocks all rumbled, the ancient earth shrank into itself. ...Then sank the serpent down in the deep.
26. So cheerless was the giant as back they rowed that for a while not a word he spoke; then again he turned the tiller of thought.

Hymir.
27. 'Now half the work shall you share with me or moor you fast our floating steed, or bear the whales to the dwellings home, all through the hollows of the wooded hills.'
28. Then the Thunderer rose, laid hold on the stem, he landed the boat with the water therein, and the ocean-swine, with the baler and oars himself he bore to the giant's home.
29. But still the Jötun, stubborn as ever, questioned again the Thunderer's might. 'I deem none strong, row he never so well, except he who has power to break my cup.'
30. Then the Storm God, swift, when it came to his hands dashed into pieces a pillar of stone: yes, sitting, he hurled the cup through the columns but whole it was borne to Hymir again.
31. At length the fair mistress with friendly words made known the secret she only knew: 'Strike at Hymir's skull, the food-filled giant's, it is harder than ever a wine cup was.'
32. Then rose to his knees the strong Lord of goats, and surrounded him with all the might of the Gods; still sound

above was the head of Hymir, shattered below was the shapely wine cup.

Hymir.

33. 'Gone already I think is my treasure, when I see the cup now cast by you kneeling.' So spoke the churl—"I can say never more,' Ale in my cauldron now are you brewed.' "

34. 'But it is yet to prove if you can bear the mighty vessel forth from our court.' —Twice in vain sought Tyr to move it; ever unstirred the cauldron stood.

35. Then the Father of Wrath laid hold on the rim and heaved the cauldron high on his head, against his heels the handles clinked, as across the hearth he strode down the hall.

36. Far had they fared before Odin's son had turned him once, to look behind and eastward saw from the landmarks forthcoming with Hymir, a war-host hundred headed.

37. From his shoulders raised he the resting cauldron, swung he Mjöllnir, death-craving hammer, and the monsters all from the mountains slew.

38. But they fared not far before the Thunderer's goat had laid him down half dead in the way; for lame in the leg was the shaft-bound steed,—it was the work of Loki, crafty in trickeries.

39. But you have heard—for who knows it better of sages learned in the lore of the Gods? —what amends made the dweller in wastes, who paid to the Thunderer both his children.

40. Swelling with might to the meeting of Gods came Thor with the cauldron which Hymir had owned, and the Holy Ones ever shall well drink ale each harvest of flax in the Sea-God's hall.

THE FORMING VERSES

NOTES

1. —Divining twigs, the oracle; see Vsp. st. 63. Aegir, a sea God, had nine daughters, and "Aegir's children" was a poetical synonym for the waves; see Grm. st. 45; Ls. And [Bray's] Introd.

4. —Tyr, the God of war, is usually called the son of Odin; see Ls. st. 38.

5. —Hymir, a frost giant, who binds the wintry sea.

7. —Egil is probably the giant mentioned in st. 39. The goats, called Tooth-gnasher and Tooth-cracker, drew Thor's chariot; st. 39.

11. —Warder. Thor always appears as the defender of mankind against the giants; see Hrbl. St. 23. In this stanza Hrod, otherwise unknown, is specified, but his name is doubtless used in a general sense.

14, —Bane of giant-wives, see Hrbl. 23.

16. —Hrungnir, a giant of great renown; Hrbl. St. 15.

23.—The Girdle is the World-serpent, called also Middle Earth's worm. He is one of Loki's children; see Vsp. st. 55, Vsp. en skamma st. 8.

24. —Fenrir, the famous Wolf; see Vsp. st. 54, Vsp. en skammu st. 8.

26. —Hymir has formed a fresh scheme for defeating Thor (Dt.). G. and others understand simply that he has turned the boat towards land.

35. —Wrath or Modi. This son is mentioned in Vm. st. 51.

39. —The dweller in wastes, or mountain giant (presumably Egil), belongs to another story of Thor's adventures tn Jötunheim; see [Bray's] Intro.

THE LAY OF THRYM

1. Wrathful was the Thunderer when he awakened and missed his hammer, the mighty Mjöllnir. His beard was quivering, his locks were shivering, —as he groped around him—the Son of Earth.

2. 'Listen now, Loki, to this I shall tell you!' —these, first of all his words, he spoke 'no being in high heaven or earth yet sees it: The God of Thunder is robbed of his hammer.'

3. Then sought they the shining halls of Freyja, and these, first of all his words, spoke Thor: 'Will you, Freyja, lend me your feather-coat, that perchance I may find my hammer?'

Freyja.

4. 'I would give it you though it were golden, still would I grant it though it were silver!' Away flew Loki, the feather-coat rustled, till he came outside the dwellings of Asgard, came within the Jötun realms.

5. Thrym sat on a mound, the lord of giants, for his greyhounds twisting golden circlets, smoothing over the manes of his steeds.

Thrym.

6. 'How do the Gods fare? how do the Elves fare? Why alone are come into Jötunheim?'

Loki.

Ill do the Gods fare, ill do the Elves fare. Speak! have you hidden the Thunderer's hammer? '

Thrym.

7. 'Yes, I have hidden the Thunderer's hammer eight miles under, deep in the earth: and never a being back shall win it till he bring me as bride fair Freyja.'

8. Away flew Loki, the feather-coat rustled, till he came outside the realms of the Jötuns, came within the gardens of the Gods. There amidst the courts the Thunderer met he, and these, first of all his words, spoke Thor.

9. 'Have you had issue meet for your labor? Tell out aloft and at length your tidings. For often when sitting a tale is broken; often when resting a lie is spoken.'

THE FORMING VERSES

Loki.
10. 'I have had toil and issue also. Thrym has your hammer, lord of giants: never a being back shall win it till he bring him as bride fair Freyja.'
11. Directly went they to find fair Freyja, and these, first of all his words, spoke Thor: 'Bind you, Freyja, in bridal linen, we two must drive into Jötunheim.'
12. Angry then was Freyja; fiercely she panted; the halls of Asgard all trembled under, burst that mighty necklace of Brisings. 'Know me to be most wanton of women if I drive with you into Jötunheim.'
13. Straight were gathered all Gods at the doomstead; Goddesses all were in speech together; and the mighty Powers upon this took counsel, how the Thunderer's hammer they should win again.
14. Spoke then Heimdal, of Gods the fairest; —even as the Wanes could he see far forward—'Come bind we Thor in bridal linen, let him wear the mighty Brisinga-men.'
15. 'Let us cause the keys to jingle under him, weeds of a woman to dangle round him, and over his breast lay ample jewels, and daintily let us hood his head.'
16. Spoke the Thunderer of Gods the sturdiest: 'Womanish then the Powers will call me if I let me be bound in bridal linen.'
17. Spoke then Loki, the son of Laufey: 'Silence, Thor! with words so witless! Soon shall the Jötuns dwell in Asgard unless you get you again your hammer.'
18. Then bound they Thor in bridal linen, also with the mighty Brisinga-men.
19. They caused the keys to jingle under him, weeds of a woman to dangle round him, and over his breast laid ample jewels and daintily they hooded his head.
20. Spoke then Loki, the son of Laufey: 'I will fare with you as your serving-maiden: we two will drive into Jötunheim.'
21. Forthwith the goats were homeward driven, sped to the traces, well must they run!

Quaked were the mountains, earth was aflame; fared Odin's son into Jötunheim.

22. Spoke then Thrym, the lord of giants: 'Stand up, Jötuns! and strew the benches! Now shall you bring me as bride fair Freyja, daughter of Njord, from Noatun.'

23. 'Golden-horned cows are found in my dwellings and oxen all tawny, the joy of the giant. I own many treasures I rule many riches, and Freyja alone to me seems lacking.'

24. Swiftly drew the day to evening, borne was the ale cup forth to the Jötuns, Thor ate an ox and eight whole salmon, with dainties all as should a damsel, three full cups of mead he guzzled.

25. Spoke then Thrym, the lord of giants, 'Did ever see damsel eat so bravely? Never have I seen one bite so boldly, nor a maiden guzzle more cups of mead!'

26. All crafty sat by the serving-maiden, who answer found to the giant's asking: 'Nothing has Freyja these eight nights eaten, so sore her yearning for Jötunheim.'

27. Stooped then Thrym beneath the veil, to kiss her, back he leapt the hall's whole length: 'Why are fair Freyja's eyes so fearful? It seems from those eyes a fire is flaming.'

28. All crafty sat by the serving-maiden, who answer found to the giant's asking: 'Not a bit has Freyja these eight nights slumbered, so sore her yearning for Jötunheim.'

29. In came the wretched sister of Jötuns and dared to beg for a bridal token: 'Take the red rings from off your fingers if you will win you my affection, my affection, all my favor!'

30. Spoke then Thrym, the lord of giants: 'Bring in the hammer, the bride to hallow. Mjöllnir lay on the knee of the maiden! Hallow us two with the hand of the Troth-Goddess!'

31. Laughed in his breast the heart of the Thunderer; strong was his soul when he spied his hammer. He first smote Thrym, the lord of giants, and all the Jötun's kindred crushed.

32. Smote he the ancient sister of Jötuns,—her who had begged for a bridal token. She got but a stroke in the place of tokens; Mjöllnir's mark and never a ring.

And so Thor won him again his hammer.

THE FORMING VERSES

NOTES

1.— Mjöllnir, the Crusher, Thor's thunder hammer; see Vm. 51, Ls. st. 57. Earth, or Jord, a wife of Odin; see Ls. st. 26, Hrbl. 56.

5. —Thrym's name, like that of other Jötuns, signifies noise; see Vm. st. 29.

12. —Necklet of Brisings. This famous mythological treasure, called Brisingamen, like many others, was won from the dwarfs; see [Bray's] Intro.

17. —Loki, see Ls., Laufey, or Leaf-isle, Loki's mother; also called Nal, or Pine-needle, by Snorri.

27. —Eyes so fearful. When Thor was angry he let his bushy brows drop over his eyes "so that you could scarce get a glimpse of them" (Snorri).

30. —Thor was called on by the old Norse peasants to bless their marriage feasts with his hammer. Troth Goddess, or Var, was guardian of oaths and plightings.

THE STORY OF SKIRNIR

Once Frey, son of Njord, had seated himself on Window-Shelf, and was gazing out over all worlds. When he looked into Jötunheim he beheld a fair maiden going from her father's hall to the garden, and at the sight of her he was seized with great sickness of heart. Now Prey's servant was called Skirnir, and Njord bade him ask speech of his master; and Skadi, wife of Njord, said:—

1. Rise, bright Skirnir! run swiftly, and plead our son to speak: ask the wise youth to answer you this, Against whom his wrath is aroused.
Skirnir.
2. If I seek for speech with him, your son, ill words I shall by chance win, if I ask the wise youth to answer me this, against whom his wrath is aroused.
(Skirnir to Frey).
3. Tell me truly, Frey, ruler of Gods, what I gladly would learn from your lips: why sit you alone in the hall, my lord, lingering the live-long day?
Frey.
4. How shall I ever confess to you, youth, the great heart's burden I bear? the Elf-light shines each day the same, but works not yet my will.
Skirnir.
5. Scarce are the longings of your love so great but I believe you can tell them to me; we were young together in days of old, we two may well trust each other.
Frey.
6. In the courts of Gymir, the frost-giant, saw I that maiden most dear to me; light shone out from her arms and then all the air and sea were shining.
7. She is dearer to me than ever was maiden to youth in days of old: but none among all the Gods and Elves has willed that we two should wed.

THE FORMING VERSES

Skirnir.
8. Give me steed to bear me safe through the dim enchanted flickering flame, and the sword which wages war of itself against the fearful Jötun Folk.
Frey.
9. Here is steed to bear you safe through the dim enchanted flickering flame, and the sword which wages war of itself, if he who bears it be bold.
Skirnir (speaking to the horse).
10. Dark it is outside! It is time, I see, to fare over the dewy fells: amid the throng of giants we shall both win through, or the awful Jötun have both.

Then Skirnir rode into Jötunheim to the dwellings of Gymir, where fierce dogs were chained up before the gate of the enclosure which surrounded Gerd's hall. He rode up to a herdsman who was sitting on a mound, and said:—

11. Speak, you herdsman, who sits on a mound and watches every way! How, for Gymir's hounds, will I ever hold speech with that Jötun's youthful maid?
Herdsman.
12. Either doomed are you, or one of the dead going forth to the halls of Hel! never a word shall you win, I see, with Gymir's goodly maid.
Skirnir.
13. A wiser choice than to whine makes he who is ready to run his race: my time was set to a certain day and my length of life decreed.
Gerd (within the hall).
14. What is the clanking and clashing of sounds which echoing I hear in our halls? Trembles the earth and before it all the courts of Gymir are shook.
A Serving-maid.
15. See! A man outside! He is sprung from his steed, which he now lets graze on the grass.

Gerd.
16. Offer him come in; let him enter our halls, let him drink the glorious mead! Yet I fear me much lest that man outside the slayer of my brother should be.

Gerd to Skirnir (who has entered).
17. Who comes, nor of Elves' nor of Gods' Folk seeming, nor yet of the all-wise Wanes? why has fared alone through the raging fire to visit the Folk in our halls?

Skirnir.
18. I come, nor of Elves' nor of Gods' Folk am I, nor yet of the all-wise Wanes; yet have I fared through the raging fire to visit the Folk in your halls.

19. Eleven apples all golden have I; these will I give you, Gerd, to win your heart that from now Frey be deemed the dearest in life.

Gerd.
20. Not ever will I take those eleven apples at the will of any being, nor will we two live, Frey and I, together while life shall last.

Skirnir.
21. Then a ring I offer you, once it was burned with Odin's youthful son; it lets fall ever eight golden rings of a like weight each ninth night.

Gerd.
22. No ring do I want, though once it was burned with Odin's youthful son. Gold is not lacking in Gymir's courts, nor my father's riches to rule.

Skirnir.
23. See you this sword, maiden, slender, rune-graven, which here I hold in my hand? Your head will I chop from off your neck, if you speak not soon your consent.

Gerd.
24. It shall never befall me to suffer force to the will of any being. I see if you meet with Gymir in war that fiercely you two will fight.

THE FORMING VERSES

Skirnir.
25. See you this sword, maiden, slender, rune-graven, which here I hold in my hand? Before its keen edge shall fall that old Giant, —your father is doomed to death.
26. With a taming wand I will touch you, maid! and win you soon to my will. I will send you far off where you shall be seen never more by the sons of men.
27. On an eagle's mound shall you sit from morn, gazing out of the world toward Hel: your food shall seem more loath than bright-hued serpent seemed ever to man among men.
28. Sight of wonder when you walk, all beings shall stare on you and the Frost Giant fix you with his eye! Known wider than Heimdal the Watchman of Gods, you shall gape through the gates of Hel.
29. Trolls shall torment you from morn till eve in the realms of the Jötun Folk, each day to the dwellings of Frost giants must you creep helpless, creep hopeless of love; you shall weeping have instead of joy, and sore burden bear with tears.
30. With a three-headed giant must you abide or lack ever husband in life. Care shall lay hold on your heart and mind, you shall waste with mourning away, as a thistle shall be which has thrust itself up in the latter season full late.
31. The Frost-hooded giant shall hold you fast beneath the doors of the dead; at the tree's roots there shall wretched thralls give you foul water of goats; and other mouthful shall you never drink, at your wish, maiden, with my will, maid.
32. Sit you down! I will further woes two-fold show you, a submerging wave of care. May madness and shrieking, bondage and yearning, burden you, with trouble and tears.
33. Angry is Odin! Angry is the Thunderer! Frey too shall hate you, I believe: you evil maiden, well have you earned the awful anger of the Gods!
34. Hear now, Jötuns, Frost-giants hear me, Suttung's sons beneath the earth, you God-Folk, too! how I ban and forbid man's love to the maiden, man's joy to the maid.
35. I went to the forest to find and fetch a magic wand of might; to a green-wood tree [Yggdrasil], and I got me there this mighty magic wand.

36. I have cut you a giant, and carved you three staves, lust and raving and rage. Even as I cut them on so can I cut them off, if by chance I have the will.
(Gerd offers him a foaming cup.)
37. Be gracious rather, youth! Take now this frosty cup filled with famous old mead. Little I thought that ever in life I should love a Waneling well.
Skirnir.
38. All my errand will I know to the end before I ride homeward hence. When will you, maiden, meet at the trysting the stalwart son of Njord?
Gerd.
39. Pine-needle is the wood of peaceful faring, we two know well the way: here shall Gerd bestow on the son of Njord her heart's love nine nights from now.

Then Skirnir rode home. Frey was standing outside, and he greeted him and asked for tidings.

Frey.
40. Speak, Skirnir! Cast not saddle from the steed, and stir not one step forward: what have you won of your will and mine in the realms of the Jötun Folk?
Skirnir.
41. Pine-needle is the wood of peaceful faring, we two know well the way: there shall Gerd bestow on the son of Njord her heart's love nine nights hence.
Frey.
42. Long is one night, long are two nights how shall I live through three! Shorter a month has seemed to me often than waiting this half night here.

THE FORMING VERSES

NOTES

Frey, see [Bray's] Introd. and Ls., st. 42. Njord, set Ls., st. 34. Window shelf, Odin's high seat. Skirnir's name means the Light-bringer.

4. —Elf-light, a name for the sun from its power over dwarfs or Elves; see Alv., St. 16.

8, 9. —The sword, see Ls., st. 42; Vsp., st. 53.

12. —Going forth to the halls of Hel, see [Bray's]Intro. to Bdr.

16. —Slayer of my brother. Frey slew the giant Beli, who was perhaps Gerd's brother; but, according to Snorri, this was after the loss of his sword, for he used a stag's horn; see Vsp., st. 53.

19. —Apples all golden. These were the property of Idun; see [Bray's] Intro. Ls.

21. —A ring, Draupnir, the dropper, which was forged for Odin by the dwarfs, and burned with Baldr; see [Bray's] Intro., Bdr., and st. 10.

27. —An eagle, Corpse-swallower, who sits at the end of heaven; Vm., st. 37.

30. —The latter season, so Dt. Hl. Others, a loft, under the roof.

31. —At the tree's roots. Presumably Yggdrasil's root stretching over Jötunheim; (Nd. D.Alt, xxx.).

33. —Thunderer. Thor is here called prince of Gods. These three Odin, Thor, and Frey are usually ranked together, and appear as the chief Gods in temple worship.

34. —Sutting, a giant of the underworld; see Hav., st. 102.

35. — A green-wood tree, see Hav., st. 150. [See Rydberg's thesis on the history of the sword as part of a grand Teutonic epic.]

36 —Giant: Icelandic thurs. The name of some object was given to each runic letter, and here the "th" would represent thurs.

37. —Waneling. Prey's father Njord was a Wane; see Ls., st. 35; Vm., st. 39.

DAY-SPRING AND MENGLÖD

PART I. THE SPELL-SONGS OF GROA

Son.
1. Wake you, Groa, wake, sweet woman, at the doors of the dead, awake! Your child, you bid me, —do you not mind you? —come to the marker of your grave.

Groa.
2. What sorrow grieves you, my only son, with what burden are overloaded, that you call your mother who is turned to dust and gone from the Folk-world forth?

Son.
3. A fearful task has that false woman set me, who fondly my father has clasped: she has sent me where none may go, to seek the joy-necklaced maiden Menglöd.

Groa.
4. Long is the faring, long are the pathways, long are the loves of men: well it may be that you gain your will, but the end must follow fate.

Son.
5. Sing me spell-songs, sweet and strong ones! Mother, shield me your child! Dead on the way I see I shall be, for I feel me too young in years.

Groa.
6. I sing you the first—well it serves, they say—which Rindr sang to Ran: be your burden too heavy, may it fall from your back and may self lead self at will.

7. I sing you the second: if by chance you stray joyless on journeys far, may the web of Wyrd be around your way and save you from shameful plight.

8. I sing you the third: if mighty streams with their waters overwhelm your life, may those floods of Hel flow back, and dry be the paths before your feet.

9. I sing you the fourth: if foes should lurk in ambush, armed for your death, be their hearts quickly toward you turned and their minds be moved to peace.

THE FORMING VERSES

10. I sing you the fifth: if men make fast a charm on the joints of your limbs, that loosening spell which I sing over your legs shall break fetters from hands and feet.

11. I sing you the sixth: if you fare over seas mightier than men do know, may wind and wave for you work your boat, and make peaceful your path over the deep.

12. I sing you the seventh: if you are assailed by frost on the icy fell, may your flesh not die in the deadly cold; be you sound in life and limb.

13. I sing you the eighth: if night overtake you, wandering on the misty way, none the more may the ghost of a Christian woman have power to work your woe.

14. I sing you the ninth: when you of necessity must stand in speech with that spear-famed giant, may words and wisdom to lips and heart in abundance be bestowed.

15. May you never be led, where danger lurks, may harm not hinder your will!

* * * * * * * * * *

At the doors I stood, on an earth-bound stone, while I sang these songs to you.

16. Child, bear with you a mother's words, let them abide in your heart! Wealth enough in life you shall win if you keep my counsel in mind.

VIKINGS BÓK

NOTES

6. —Rindr, another name for Odin as husband of the giantess Rind (Bdr., st. 11), who is here called Ran. Odin long wooed her in vain, and won her at last by enchantments (Saxo Grammaticus); cf. the same use of the masculine and feminine forms in Fjorgynn and Fjorgyn; see Ls., st, 26. [William Reaves gives Rindr as the name of Vali's mother.]

7. —Wyrd or Urd, the Goddess of fate; see Vip., 20.

8. —Floods of Hel, here called Horn and Rud, not mentioned in the list of the rivers which flow from Roaring-kettle; see Grin., st. 28, 29.

13. —Ghosts of Christian women. This line must have been written in Heathen days, as Christianity is regarded as a mysterious power of evil.

14. —That spear-famed giant must be Much-wise, the warder of Menglöd's halls.

PART II. THE SAYINGS OF MUCH-WISE

1. Stood Day-spring outside the walls, and saw loom high the Jötuns' home.
Day-spring.
What monster is that who guards the threshold, and prowls round the perilous flames?
Much-wise.
2. Whom do you seek? Of whom are in search? What, friendless being, would you learn? Back wander now on your dewy way; not here is your haven, lone one!
Day-spring.
3. What monster is that who guards the threshold and bids not welcome to wanderers? Lacking all seemly speech were you born; now, speaker, hasten you home!
Much-wise.
4. Much-wise I am called, for I am wise in mind, though none too free with my food. Here in the courts shall you never come; get you from here like a wolf on your way!
Day-spring.
5. Longs the lover again for the light of his eyes, with his sweet-heart back in sight: glowing are the walls of that golden hall; I would gladly make here my home.
Much- wise.
6. Tell me, bold youth, from whom you are sprung, son of what being were born?
Day-spring.
They call me Wind-cold, the son of Spring-cold, whose father was Fierce-cold named.
7. Now answer me, Much-wise, this that I ask and gladly would learn from your lips: who here does rule and hold in power the wealth and wondrous halls?
Much-wise.
8. There is one called Menglöd, who of her mother was born to Sleep-thorn's son: it is she does rule and hold in power the wealth and wondrous halls.

Day-spring.
9. Now answer me, Much-wise, this that I ask and gladly would learn from your lips: what is that gate called? Never among Gods was more fearful barrier found.

Much-wise.
10. Sounding-clanger the gate is called, wrought by three sons of Sun-blind. Fast is the chain to each wanderer who seeks to lift that door from the latch.

Day-spring.
11. Now answer me, Much-wise, this that I ask and gladly would learn from your lips: what is that wall named? Never among Gods was more fearful barrier found.

Much-wise.
12. Guest-crusher it is called; from the Clay-giant's limbs I built that barrier myself: so strong have I set it that firm it will stand, forever while life shall last.

Day-spring.
13. Now answer me, Much-wise, this that I ask and gladly would learn from your lips: what is that tree, which far and wide, spreads limbs over every land?

Much-wise.
14. It is the tree of Mimir, but no man knows by what roots it rises to heaven: it will fall at last by what least one sees, for not fire nor weapons will wound it.

Day-spring.
15. Now answer me, Much-wise, this that I ask and gladly would learn from your lips: what befalls the fruit of that famous tree which neither fire nor weapons will wound?

Much-wise.
16. The fruit thereof must be laid on the fire for the good of travailing women; they shall then come out who had been within. To mankind it is the giver of life.

Day-spring.
17. Now answer me, Much-wise, this that I ask and gladly would learn from your lips: what cock sits perched in that lofty tree, who is glistening all with gold?

THE FORMING VERSES

Much- wise.
18. Wood-snake he is called, who storm-bright sits in the boughs of Mimir's Tree: with one long dread he galls beyond measure giant and giant-wife.
Day-spring.
19. Now answer me, Much-wise, this that I ask and gladly would learn from your lips: what fierce hounds watch in front of the courts ravening and roaming around?
Much-wise.
20. One is called Greed, the other Glutton, if by chance you would hear: mighty warders they are who watch, for indeed until the Powers perish.
Day-spring.
21. Now answer me, Much-wise, this that I ask and gladly would learn from your lips: is there never a being may pass within while the fierce hounds are held in sleep?
Much-wise.
22. Division of sleep was ever their lot since it was given them to guard: sleeps one by night, and the other by day, and none who comes may win through.
Day-spring.
23. Now answer me, Much-wise, this that I ask and gladly would learn from your lips: is there no food which man can find them and dart through the doors while they feast?
Much-wise.
24. There lie two wings in the Wood-snake's sides, if by chance you would hear: this alone is that food which if man can find, he shall dare through the doors while they feast.
Day-spring.
25. Now answer me, Much-wise, this that I ask and gladly would learn from your lips: is there no weapon to strike the Wood-snake down to the halls of Hel?
Much-wise.
26. It is the Wounding Wand which Loki plucked beneath the doors of the dead: Sinmara keeps it with nine fast locks, shut in Sea-lover's chest.

Day-spring.
27. Now answer me, Much-wise, this that I ask and gladly would learn from your lips: comes he ever again, who goes to seek, and craves to win that wand?
Much-wise.
28. He shall come again who goes to seek and craves to win that wand; if he brings the treasure which none does own, the gold-bright Goddess to please.
Day-spring.
29. Now answer me, Much-wise, this that I ask and gladly would learn from your lips: is there no treasure which man can take to rejoice that pale-hued giantess?
Much-wise.
30. In its quill must you bear the bright sickled plume, which was taken from Wood-snake's tail, and give to Sinmara before she will grant you that weapon of war to use.
Day-spring.
31. Now answer me, Much-wise, this that I ask and gladly would learn from your lips: what hall is there, all girt around by enchanted flickering flames?
Much-wise.
32. Glowing it is called and long must it quiver as though on the spear's point set; far tidings only, throughout all time, man hears of this wondrous hall.
Day-spring.
33. Now answer me, Much-wise, this that I ask and gladly would learn from your lips: what beings, born of the Gods have built what I saw inside the court?
Much-wise.
34. Uni and Iri, Bari and Ori, Var and Vegdrasil, Dori and Uri, Delling, Atvard, Lidskjalf and Loki were these.
Day-spring.
35. Now answer me, Much-wise, this that I ask and gladly would learn from your lips: what hill is that on whose height I see that wondrous Woman resting?

THE FORMING VERSES

Much-wise.
36. It is the Hill of Healing; long has it held, for the sick and sorrowful, joy: each woman is healed who climbs its height, even of year-long ills.
Day-spring.
37. Now answer me, Much-wise, this that I ask and gladly would learn from your lips: who are the maidens, at Menglöd's knees all gathered in peace together?
Much-wise.
38. They are spirits, Sheltering, Shielding giants, Guarding warriors in war, Bright and Tender, Merry and Peaceful, Gentle, Generous maids.
Day-spring.
39. Now answer me, Much-wise, this that I ask and gladly would learn from your lips: will they shelter all who make offering to them, if need thereof arise?
Much-wise.
40. Those Wise Ones shelter where men make offering in the sacred altar-stead: no peril so mighty can man befall but they save him soon from need.
Day-spring.
41. Now answer me, Much-wise, this that I ask and gladly would learn from your lips: is there never being in the world may lie in Menglöd's soften arms sleeping?
Much-wise.
42. There is never being in the world may lie in Menglöd's soften arms sleeping but Day-spring, to whom of old was given that sun-bright maiden as bride.
Day-spring.
43. Fling open the door, make wide the gate, Day-spring is here, behold! Yet hasten you first, and find if in truth Menglöd longs for my love.
Much-wise to Menglöd.
44. Hearken, Menglöd, a guest is here! Come you this stranger behold! The hounds are joyous, the hall has opened. it is Day-spring, well I see!

Menglöd.
45. Now may fierce ravens tear yours eyes out, high on the gallows hanging, if falsely you say that from far away comes Day-spring here to my halls!
To Day-spring.
46. Where have you come, when made your way, how do your home-folk call you? Show Folk and name before I know that to you in truth I have been betrothed.
Day-spring.
47. Day-spring am I, the child of Sun-bright, by winds on my chill way wafted; the doom of Wyrd may no being withstand even though measured wrongly.
Menglöd.
48. Now welcome are you! My will is won; with greeting comes the kiss. Never sweeter is sight of heart's desire than when one brings love to another.
49. Long have I sat on the Hill of Healing, awaiting you day by day; till that I looked for at length is come, —you are back, youth, here in my halls.
50. Yearnings had I often for your heart, and you did long for my love: now all is made sure, we two shall share together the days of time.

THE FORMING VERSES

NOTES

5. —*This strophe, like 49, suggests that Svipdagr and Menglöd have met before.*

10.—*Solblind or Sun-blinded must be a dwarf name for one who, like All-wise (st. 35), fears the light, and whose children are forgers like Brokk and Sindri; see Vsp. 37, Grm. st. 43, and [Bray's] Introd.*

12. —*The Clay-giant or Leirbrimir. From the giant Ymir or Brimir (Vm., st. 21) was made the whole framework of earth, and the expression is only a poetical term for the solid ground.*

14. —*The tree of Mimir, Yggdrasil; see Vsp. 19, 29; Vm. 45. Mimir's well, like that of Wyrd, was situated beneath it, and here, in Giant-home, the tree would be called his.*

16. —*Giver of life, or, according to another reading, the Fate-tree, as in Vsp st. 2.*

17. —*Wood-snake, a poetical name for bird. This cock may be Golden Comb, who wakes the Gods at the coming of the giants (Vsp., st. 43), and is hence the dread of giant and giant-wife, or, more probably, Fjalar (Vsp., st. 42), who sits "in the roosting tree," and sounds the first note of doom. The names of Surt and Sinmara, found in the text, are used in a general sense.*

20. —*Mighty warders, or, if another reading is taken, eleven warders there are who watch, named perhaps in st. 34.*

26. —*The Wounding Wand must be the mistletoe with which Baldr was slain. Snorri tells us that it grew to the west of Vallhall; see Bdr., st. 9. Sinmara: This giantess is only mentioned in st. 18, where she is coupled with Surt, as though his wife.*

28. —*Gold-bright Goddess. A poetical term for woman.*

30. —*Quill, a suggestion for lutr, which means case or box; but whose significance is here doubtful.*

35. —*Dori, Ori, and Delling are dwarfs (see Vsp., st. 15; Vm., st. 25); Loki, the God. The others are unknown; their names do not seem to indicate their powers like those of st. 38.*

47. —*The doom of Wyrd, see Spell-songs, st. 4.*

GREYBEARD AND THOR

As Thor was journeying from the Eastern Land of the Jötuns he came to a seaway. On the other side was a ferryman with his boat.

Thor.
1. What boy of boys are you who is on that side of the sound standing?

Greybeard.
2. Tell me rather what peasant of peasants so calls across the wave.

Thor.
3. Row me over! A meal this morn I'll pay you, choicer fare you shall never find you. Here on my back there hangs a basket; in peace I ate, myself, before I started, herrings and goat's flesh, and still am I satisfied.

Greybeard.
4. As a morning's work you do boast your meal; but you are not all forseeing: filled with care at home are your kindred, dead I believe is your mother.

Thor.
5. Worst of all tidings are you telling, when you say to me now that dead is my mother.

Greybeard.
6. At least you look not like one who owns a lot of three fair lands; bare-legged you stand, clad like a beggar, and not even leggings have you on.

Thor.
7. Steer the boat nearer! I will show you a haven. Who owns that boat which by the bow you hold?

Greybeard.
8. Battle-wolf bade me—wise-counselled hero, who dwells in Counsel-Isle Sound—to keep it and ferry not rogues or robbers but the worthy and those I know well. Now shall you tell me your name if you gladly would come fare over the flood.

THE FORMING VERSES

Thor.
9. Were I outlawed, yet my name would I tell you, Hail my Folk. I am son of Odin, the brother of Meili, and father of Magni, Gods' Strength-wielder; you speak with Thor. Gladly would I know now your name and kinship.
Greybeard.
10. They call me Grey-beard; it is seldom I care to hide my own name from any.
Thor.
11. Why should you not show your name, except you have cause of strife with your foemen?
Greybeard.
12. Have I cause, against such as you will I hold my life unless I be doomed.
Thor.
13. Sore shame it would be to wet my burden in wading so through the water toward you. Those mocking words would I pay you, child, could I but reach that side of the sound now.
Greybeard.
14. Here I stand and await you! Never met you with sturdier hero since Hrungnir was slain.
Thor.
15. Do tell how we once fought, I and Hrungnir, that hard-hearted giant whose head was rock-hewn? Yet did he fall and bow before me. What, the while, were you working, Greybeard?
Greybeard.
16. I dwelled with Wary-wise five whole winters in the island called All-green. Battles we fought there and felled the doomed, much daring, and wiling women.
Thor.
17. Got you good or woe from those wives of your winning?
Greybeard.
18. Merry wives had we owned had they borne them wisely; shrewd wives, had they shown them true: all out of sand they spun them ropes and dug from the deep dales earth. Yet slyest was I, who with seven sisters slept, and won all their liking and love. What, the while, were you working, Thunderer?'

Thor.
19. Slew I Thiazi, son of All-wielder, strong-souled Jötun, and flung his eyes up where men shall behold in the shining heavens the tokens great of my deeds hereafter. What, the while, were you working, Greybeard?
Greybeard.
20. I had dealings in love with the dark witch-riders, from their husbands I wiled them away: stout giant seemed Hlebard till his wand he gave me and I wiled him out of his wits.
Thor.
21. Then spite for those goodly gifts you gave?
Greybeard.
22. Let one oak take what it scrapes off another, and let each man seek his own. What, the while, were you working, Thunderer?
Thor.
23. Slew I the evil wives of Jötuns, far in the east, as they fled to the mountains: were they all left in the land of the living, huge would have been now the host of giants, and never a man would there be in Middle Earth. What, the while, were you working, Greybeard?
Greybeard.
24. In the Land of the Slain I warred and stirred up princes to strife without peace. Odin has earls who fall on the battlefield, Thor has the breed of thralls.
Thor.
25. Unfairly would you divide the slain among Gods if power too great were given you!
Greybeard.
26. Strength enough has the Thunderer, nothing of daring; from fear and faintness of heart you were thrust, I see, in a glove-thumb once, and scarce could deem yourself Thor: lest Fjalar should hear you, for fright you dare not sneeze nor stir a hair.
Thor.
27. Greybeard, you craven! Could I but stretch over the sound I would smite you soon into Hel-home.

THE FORMING VERSES

Greybeard.
28. Why should you stretch over the seaway and smite me? No reason have we for wrath. What, the while, were you working, Thunderer?

Thor.
29. Eastward held I the flood of Ifing against the sons of Svarang the Whelmer; with stones they harassed me but small gain got they and first were found to ask peace of foemen. What, the while, were you working, Greybeard?

Greybeard.
30. In the East I dallied with one, my chosen; I played with that linen-fair lass, kept secret trysting, and gladdened the gold-bright maiden, merry in the game.

Thor.
31. Glad meetings of love had you there with maidens?

Greybeard.
32. Need had I then of help from Thor, to have kept that linen-fair lass.

Thor.
33. Gladly would I give it you, could I but get there.

Greybeard.
34. Gladly would I now put trust in your faith, were you not wanting to betray me.

Thor.
35. No heel biter I, like an old shoe in spring-time!

Greybeard.
36. What, the while, were you working, Thunderer?

Thor.
37. Slew I berserk-wives in the Isle of Aegir; vile things wrought they, all men-folk wiling.

Greybeard.
38. A base deed then were you doing, Thunderer waging war with women!

Thor.
39. She-wolves were they, and scarcely women. My ships laid up, on the shore they shattered, with clubs they threatened me, Thialfi chased they. What, the while, were you working, Greybeard?

Greybeard.
40. To raise the war flag and redden the spear, here I came in the host.
Thor.
41. Would tell how with hate you came to harm us?
Greybeard.
42. Let a ring make atonement as the daysmen allotted, who sought to set us at peace.
Thor.
43. Where did you learn those scornful speeches? Never were words more wounding said me.
Greybeard.
44. I learnt them once from ancient beings who dwell in the hills of home.
Thor.
45. Fair name for landmarks to call them home-hills!
Greybeard.
46. It is even as I think concerning such things.
Thor.
47. Sorely your skill in words should serve you, could I but wade to you through the water. Louder, I see, than a wolf will you howl if by chance you get a stroke from my hammer.
Greybeard.
48. Sif has a lover, your wife at home, are you not eager to meet him? That a deed of daring now must you do, a work which well befits you.
Thor.
49. Faint-heart! Speak you as worst it seems, by the counsel of your lips; for I believe you lie!
Greybeard.
50. Truly I see that my words are spoken: too slow are you in your travelling. Far on your way had you fared now, Thor, if you had but gone in disguise.
Thor.
51. Greybeard, you craven! Too long you delay me.
Greybeard.
52. I had never seen boatman would hinder the way of Thor, the Thunderer of Gods.

THE FORMING VERSES

Thor.
53. Now will I counsel you; come in your boat hither; fetch Magni's father, and cease we from mocking.

Greybeard.
54. Hurry you now away from the sound! The ferry to you is refused.

Thor.
55. Show me a path then, since you will not ferry me over the flood between us.

Greybeard.
56. It is little to withhold, it is far to fare a while to the stock and the stone: so shall you hold to the left-hand path, till you arrive on the Land of Men; there will Earth meet her son and show him the way of his Folk to the realms of Odin.

Thor.
57. Shall I to-day reach the dwellings of Odin?

Greybeard.
58. With weariness and toil when the dew is wet at sunrise, I see, you will win them.

Thor.
59. Short be our speech now, with but jeering you answer. When we meet next I'll pay you for denying me passage.

Greybeard.
60. Hurry you now away where the fiends may seize you, body and soul!

VIKINGS BÓK

NOTES

[William Reaves suggests, following Rydberg, that Greybeard is really a servant boy in disguise, and underneath it all, Loki.]

2. Prose. Presumably Odin in disguise; see [Bray's] Intro.

3. —Herrings and goat's flesh. For Thor as a fisherman, see Hym., st. 17-25. He usually ate his goats for supper, and restored them to life in the morning; see [Bray's] Intro. Hym. This rendering of hafra seems more probable than the more common alternative oats; Thor's meal of goat's flesh was famous, and a burlesque like the present poem would be incomplete without some allusion to it.

8. —Battle-wolf, meaning himself, the patron of war.

9. —Meili. Nothing is known concerning this son of Odin. Magni or Might, see Vm., st. 51.

10. —Greybeard. Odin's preferred disguise was that of a grey-bearded old man.

11. —Cause of strife, see G. gloss.

14. —Hrungnir. The slaying of this giant was one of Thor's famous deeds; see Hym., st. 16.

16. —Wary-wise, unknown.

19. —Thiazi. See Ls., st. 50, and Introd.; Vsp. en skamma, st. 3.

26. —Fjalar, a giant, otherwise known as Utgard-loki; see [Bray's] Intro.

29. —Ifing. The name is not mentioned in the text, but it may be assumed that the river is that which flowed between the realms of Gods and giants; see Vm. 16.

34. —Wanting to betray me. This rendering seems justified by the ensuing st.; see [Bray's] Intro.

37. —Aegir, here called by his other name Hler.

44. —Hills of home, the ancestral graves.

48. —Sif's lover, is Loki; see Ls., st. 54.

56. —Earth, or Jord, who is here called Fjorgyn, is one of Odin's wives; see Ls., ft. 26.

58. When the dew is wet, B's interpretation; about that time, G.

THE SONG OF RIG

It is told in the sagas of old that a certain God called Heimdal was passing on his way along the sea shore when he came to a farm. He entered, calling himself Rig according to the story which so relates:

I. THE BIRTH OF THRALL.

1. Once walked, it is said, the green ways along, mighty and ancient, strong and vigorous, a God most glorious; striding, Rig.
2. Ever on he went in the middle of the way, till he came to a house with door unclosed. He entered straight; there was fire on the floor and an old couple sitting by the hearth, Great-grandfather and mother in ancient guise.
3. Well knew Rig how to give them counsel, he sat him down in the middle of the floor, with the home-folk upon either side.
4. Great-grandmother fetched a coarse-baked loaf, all heavy and thick and crammed with husk: she bore it forth in the middle of the dish, with broth in a bowl, and laid the meal.
5. Then Rig uprose, prepared to rest; —well he knew how to give them counsel—he laid him down in the middle of the bed and the home-folk split upon either side. So he tarried three nights together, then on he strode in the middle of the road while three times three moons were gliding by.
6. Great-grandmother bore a swarthy boy; with water they sprinkled him, called him Thrall. Directly he grew and well he prospered, but rough were his hands with wrinkled skin, with knuckles knotty and fingers thick; his face was ugly, his back was humpy, his heels were long. . . Straightway began he to prove his strength, with bast fiber a-binding loads a-making, he bore home branches the livelong day.
7. There came to the dwellings a wandering maid, with wayworn feet, and sunburned arms, with down-bent nose,— the Bond-maid named.

8. She sat her down in the middle of the floor; beside her sat the son of the house: they chatted and whispered, their bed preparing—Thrall and Bond-maid—the long day through.

9. Joyous lived they and reared their children. So they called them: Brawler, Cowherd, Boor and Horsefly, Lewd and Lustful, Stout and Stumpy, Sluggard, Swarthy, Lout and Leggy. They fashioned fences, they dung spread the meadows, swine they herded, goats they tended and turf they dug.

10. Daughters were there, —Leggy and Cloggy, Lumpy-leggy, and Eagle-nose, Whiner, Bondwoman, Oaken-peggy, Tatter-coat and the Crane-shanked maid. There are come the generations of thralls.

II. THE BIRTH OF CHURL.

11. Ever on went Rig the straight roads along till he came to a dwelling with door unclosed; he entered straight; there was fire on the floor; Grandfather and Grandmother owned the house.

12. The home-folk sat there hard at work; by them stood on the floor a box; hewed the husband wood for a warp-beam;
trim his beard and the locks over his brow, but mean and scanty the shirt he wore.

13. The wife sat by him plying her spinning staff, swaying her arms to weave the cloth, with hood on her head and smock on her chest, studs on her shoulders, and scarf on her neck.

14. Well knew Rig how to give them counsel; he sat him down in the middle of the floor, and the home-folk split upon either side.

15. Grandmother set forth plenteous dishes; cooked was the calf, of dainties best. Then Rig uprose prepared to rest. —Well he knew how to give them counsel—he laid him down in the middle of the bed and the home-folk split upon either side.

16. So he tarried three nights together, then on he strode in the middle of the road while thrice three moons were gliding by.

THE FORMING VERSES

17. A child had Grandmother, Churl they called him, and sprinkled with water and swathed in linen, rosy and ruddy, with sparkling eyes. He grew and prospered, and directly began he to break in oxen, to shape the harrow, to build him houses and barns to raise him, to fashion carts and follow the plough.

18. Then home they drove with a key-hung maiden in goat-skin kirtle, named Daughter-in-Law. They wed her to Churl in her bridal linen: the two made ready, their wealth sharing, kept house together, and joyous lived.

19. Children reared they so they called them: Youth and Hero, Thane, Smith, Yeoman, Broad-limb, Peasant, Sheaf-beard, Neighbor, Farmer, Speaker and Stubbly-beard.

20. By other names were the daughters called: Dame, Bride, Lady, Gay, and Gaudy, Maid, Wife, Woman, Bashful, Slender. Then are come the kindreds of churls.

III. THE BIRTH OF EARL.

21. Still on went Rig the straight roads along till he came to a hall whose gates looked south. Pushed was the door to, a ring in the post set: he forthwith entered the rush-strewn room.
Each other eyeing, the home-folk sat there—Father and Mother,—twirling their fingers. There was the husband, string a-twining, shafting arrows and shaping bows: and there was the wife over her fair arms wondering, smoothing her linen, stretching her sleeves. A high-peaked coif and a breast-brooch wore she, trailing robes and a blue-tinged blouse. Her brow was brighter, her breast was fairer, her throat was whiter than driven snow.

22. Well knew Rig how to give them counsel; he sat him down in the middle of the floor, and the home-folk split upon either side.

23. Then took Mother a figured cloth, white, of linen, and covered the table; thereafter took she a fine-baked loaf, white, of wheat and covered the cloth: next she brought forth plenteous dishes, set with silver, and spread the table with

brown-fried bacon and roasted birds. There was wine in a vessel and rich-wrought goblets; they drank and reveled while day went by.

24. Well knew Rig how to give them counsel; he rose before long and prepared his couch: he laid him down in the middle of the bed, and the home-folk split upon either side.

25. So he tarried three nights together; then on he strode in the middle of the road while thrice three moons were gliding by.

26. Then Mother had a boy; she swathed him in silk, and with water sprinkled him; called him Earl. Light were his locks, and fair his cheeks, flashing his eyes like a serpent's shone.

27. Grew Earl forthwith in the halls and began to swing the shield, to fit the string, to bend the bow, to shaft the arrow, to hurl the dart, to shake the spear, to ride the horse, to loose the hounds, to draw the sword, and to swim the stream.

28. Forth from the thicket came Rig a-striding, Rig a-striding, and taught him runes, his own name gave him, —as son he claimed him, and bade him hold the ancestral fields, —the ancestral fields—and the ancient home.

29. Then on rode Earl through the murky wood, through the frosty fells till he reached a hall. His shaft he shook, his shield he brandished, his steed he galloped, his sword he drew; war he wakened, the field he reddened, the doomed he slew, and won him lands—till alone he ruled over eighteen halls. Gold he scattered and gave to all men treasures and trinkets and slender-ribbed horses; wealth he strewed and sundered rings.

30. Along dewy roads his messengers drove till the hall they reached where Ruler dwelt. A daughter owned he, dainty fingered, fair and skillful, Erna called.

31. They wooed her and brought her home a-driving; to Earl they wed her in veil fine-woven: husband and wife lived happy together, their children grew and life enjoyed.

THE FORMING VERSES

IV. THE BIRTH OF KING.

32. Heir was the eldest, Child the second, Babe, Successor, Inheritor, Boy, Descendent, Offspring, Son, Youth, Kinsman; Kon the kingly was youngest born.

33. Directly grew up the sons of Earl; games they learned, and sports and swimming, taming horses, round shields bending, war shafts smoothing, ash spears shaking; but King the youngest alone knew runes, runes eternal and runes of life. Yet more he knew, —how to shelter men, to blunt the sword-edge and calm the sea: he learned bird language, to quench the fire flame, heal all sorrows and soothe the heart; strength and might of eight he owned.

34. Then he strove in runes with Rig, the Earl, crafty wiles he used and won, so gained his heritage, held the right so Rig to be called and runes to know.

35. Young King rode once through thicket and wood, shooting arrows and slaying birds, till spoke a crow, perched lone on a bough: 'Why will you so kill birds, young King? It would fit you rather to ride on horses, to draw the sword and to slay the foe.

36. 'Dan and Damp have dwellings goodlier, homesteads fairer than you do hold; and well they know the keel to ride, the sword to prove and wounds to strike.' ...

NOTES

Heimdal. —See Vsp. en skamma, st. 14; Grm. 13 and Vsp., st. 1, where men are called his children. Rig or King. —A Celtic word.

6. —Sprinkled him with water, see Hav., st. 157. Thrall, the lowest class, who were little better than slaves.

7. —Wandering. The other brides (st. 18 and 30) came, not on foot, but driving to their husbands.

17. —Churl or karl, the free-born peasant proprietor.

21. —Pushed to: Icelandic hnigin, is usually rendered open in this passage, but Vigfusson's, the door was down or shut, suggests a contrast to the humbler dwellings; st. 2, 11. The ring was for the visitor to "tirl" at, as in old ballads.

30. —Erna. No satisfactory meaning has been suggested for this name.

32. —Kon is the masculine of kona, a woman. It is a word only found in poetry applied to men of gentle or royal birth. The poet plays upon its resemblance to konungr, a king, and suggests a false derivation from kon and ungr, the young in order to show that Kon rose to the highest rank and became Rig, the king; st. 34.

33, line 2. —Transposed from 32. For the power of runes, see Hav. st. 145-163 and [Bray's] Introd.

36. —Dan and Damp appear as Danish kings in the historical sagas. The end of this poem is missing, which tells of Kon's descendants, and probably of his invasion and conquest of Denmark.

THE LAY OF HYNDLA

Freyja.
1. Wake, maid of maidens, friend, awaken, sister Hyndla, in a rock-hole biding! Comes the gloom of dusk, we two together must ride to Valhöll, the Holy dwelling.
2. The War-father bid we be mild in his mood, who grants and gives to his followers gold; he gave to Hermod a helmet and armor coat and to Sigmund gave a sword to take.
3. To some grants he wealth, to his children war-fame, word-skill to many and wisdom to men: fair winds to sea-farers, song-craft to skalds, and might of manhood to many a warrior.
4. To Thor will I offer and this will I ask him, to bear him truly ever toward you, even though foe of the wives of Jötuns.
5. Now of your wolves take one from the stall and swift let him run by the side of my boar.

Hyndla.
No! unwilling is your swine, to tread the Gods' way, nor will I burden my noble beast.
6. False are you, Freyja! you gladly would tempt me; your eyes betray you; you turn ever to where on the Dead's path your lover is with you, Ottar the youthful, Instein's son.

Freyja.
7. Dull are you, Hyndla! I believe you are dreaming, when you deem my lover is here on the Dead's road, where Golden-bristle, the boar, is glowing, the swine of battle which once they made me, Dain and Nabbi, the crafty dwarfs.
8. Let us now strive in our saddles sitting, and hold converse over the long lines of kings, heroes all who are come from the Gods.
9. Ottar the youthful, and Angantyr on this have wagered their wealth of gold; of necessity must I help the youthful hero to hold the heritage after his fathers.
10. He built me an altar with stone overlaid; like glass all split is that rock with fire, for he reddened it often with the fresh blood of oxen; indeed to the Goddesses Ottar was true.

11. Come now let ancient kinsman be numbered, and let be told the long lines of men: who is of Skjoldungs, who of Skilfings, who is of Athlings, who of Ynglings, who is freeborn, who is gentle born, choicest of all the men under Midgard?
Hyndla.
(Ottar's Folk.)
12. You are Ottar, born of Instein; Instein came from Alf the Old, Alf was from Wolf, Wolf from Seafarer, and Seafarer sprang from Swan the Red.
13. You had a mother shining in jewels, Hledis, I see, she was named, the priestess; her father was Frodi, and Friaut her mother. All of this Folk among lords are reckoned.
14. Hildigunn was the mother of Friautchild was she of Svafa and Sea-king. All this generation is yours Ottar the Simple! Would you know further, and what?
15. Klyp's son Ketil was spouse of Hildigun; he was the father of your mother's mother. Older than Karl yet was Prodi, but Alf was of all the eldest born.
16. Next came Nanna, the daughter of Nokkvir; her son was your father's brother by wedlock. Old is that kindship, still on will I tell you, for all this Folk is yours, Ottar the Simple.
17. Isolf and Osolf were sons of Olmod, and born of Skurhild, daughter of Skekkil. You shall reckon back to many a chieftain. All this Folk is yours Ottar the Simple!
(Halfdan's Folk.)
18. Far back was Ali, mightiest of men: Halfdan before him highest of Skjoldungs, whirled were his deeds round the skirts of heaven, great wars of nations the chieftains waged.
19. He joined him to Eymund, highest of heroes; Sigtrygg slew with the icy sword-edge, wedded Almveig, loftiest of ladies; so he begat him sons eighteen.
20. Onward are the Skjoldungs, onward the Skilfings, onward are the Athlings, then the Ynglings, then are freeborn, then are gentle born, all the choicest of men under Midgarth. All this Folk is yours, Ottar the Simple;
21. Dag's wife was Thora, mother of warriors; reared in that generation were the mightiest heroes, Fradmar and Gyrd, and

THE FORMING VERSES

both the Wolf-cubs, Josurmar, Am, and Alf the Old. Would you know further, and what?

(The Berserks.)

22. Born in Bolm in the eastern land were Arngrim's sons and Eyfora's; woes unnumbered the berserks worked, like the faring of fire over land and sea.

23. Hervard, Hjorvard, Hrani, Angantyr, Bui and Brami, Barri and Reifnir, Tind and Tyrfing, and Haddungs two. All this Folk is yours, Ottar the Simple!

24. Gunnar Battle-wall, Grim Strongminded, Thorir Iron shield, Wolf the Gaper; Brod and Horvi, once I knew them, both in the train of Hrolf the Old.

(The Volsung Folk.)

25. Given to the Gods were the warrior sons, all the children of Jörmunrek, the kinsman of Sigurd—list to my saga!—Fear of Nations, who Fafnir slew.

26. That ruler was born of the Folk of Volsungs, and Hjordis came, his mother, of Hraudungs, and Eylimi, her sire, of Athlings. All this Folk is yours, Ottar the Simple!

27. Gunnar and Hogni were sons of Gjuki; Gudrun their sister, was to increase his offspring; but not of their kin was Guthorm Battle-snake, though of the two he was held the brother. All this generation is yours, Ottar the Simple!

28. Best was Haki of Hvedna's children; the father of Hvedna was Hjorvard.

(Folk of Harald War-tooth.)

29. Born from Aud was Harald War-tooth, son of Hrderik, Slinger of Rings. Aud Deep-thoughted was Ivar's daughter, and Randver the son of Radbard born. All this Folk is yours, Ottar the Simple!

*   *   *   *   *   *   *   *   *   *

Freyja.

30. To my boar now bear the ale of memory, so shall he tell forth all this tale when the third morn comes, and with Angantyr he shall trace back the mighty men of their Folk.

Hyndla.
31. Hurry away there! for I gladly would sleep, and few fair words shall you win from me. You wander forth, good friend, at nights like a she-goat straying bold among bucks.

32. Yearning ever you have followed Odd; many a sweetheart has slept in yours arms. You wander forth, good friend, at nights like a she-goat straying bold among bucks.

Freyja.
33. I will strike fire about you, giantess, so that unburnt you hurry not hereafter.

Hyndla.
You wander forth, good friend, at nights like a she-goat straying bold among bucks.

34. Behold! all around us the earth is flaming! Many must render their lives as ransom. Bear now the ale-cup to Ottar's hand, all mingled with poison and omens of ill. You wander forth, good friend, at nights like a she-goat straying bold among bucks.

Freyja.
35. The word of yours omen shall work no evil, though you curse, vile wife of Jötuns; sweet shall the mouthful be that Ottar drinks, for I pray all the Powers to shield him well.

THE FORMING VERSES

NOTES

2. *Hermod belongs to some lost tradition. He appears now as a God and now as a hero. In the Prose Edda he is the son of Odin (see [Bray's] Intro. Bdr.); in the old English poem of Beowulf he is a Danish King, mighty and beneficent in his youth, but a bloodthirsty tyrant when old, who is deserted by his subjects. Sigmund, father of Sigurd (st. 25). At a wedding feast Odin entered and thrust his sword into a tree from which only Sigmund, the Gods' favorite, could draw it.*

3. *—Song-craft to skalds, see Hav., st. 105, 139.*

6. *—The Dead's way: A road by which the dead warriors went to Valhöll. Ottar: The story of Freyja's human lover Ottar or Odd is told by Snorri.*

7. *—The boar: Frey owned the boar called Golden-bristle, which was forged by the dwarfs; see [Bray's] Intro. Grm. Freyja, according to Snorri, rode on a cat. Dain, the Dead one, is mentioned in Vsp.*

9. *—Gold is here called foreign metal. Icelandic Valsk; English Welsh originally meant foreign.*

11.*—Skjoldings, etc., see [Bray's] Intro. for these traditional Folk names.*

18.*—Halfdan, a mythical King of Denmark.*

19.*—Eymund, King of Novgorod, father of Almveig (Skaldskm).*

21. *—Dag, son of Halfdan, father of Arngrim (st. 22).*

22-23. *—The story of Angantyr and the famous berserks is told in Hervarar Saga. and Orvar Odds Saga .*

24.*—Hrolf, probably Half, a famous King of Gauta-land, and hero of Halfs Saga.*

25.*—Jörmunrek, the heroicised Ermanric, King of the Goths in the fourth century. Sigurd, the hero of the Volsunga Saga, and later Niebelungenlied.*

27.*—Gjuki, of Niflung Folk, a King of the Burgundians. Guthorm, his stepson, slew Sigurd at the desire of Brynhild.*

29. *—Harald War-tooth, a King of Denmark. Hruerik, a King of Sweden, husband of Aud. The saga of these mythical personages is told in Sugubrot and by Saxo Grammaticus.*

31. *A she-goat: The name of the mythical goat Heidrun (Grm., st. 25) is here used in a general sense.*

BALDR'S DREAMS

1. Straight were gathered all Gods at the doomstead, Goddesses all were in speech together; and the mighty Powers over this took counsel,—why to Baldr came dreams foreboding.

2. Up rose Odin the ancient creator; he laid the saddle on gliding Sleipnir, and downward rode into Misty Hel. Met him a hound from a cavern coming;

3. All its breast was blood-splattered, long it bayed at the Father of Spells. Onward he rode, the Earth's way rumbled, to the lofty hall of Hel came Odin.

4. Round he rode to a door on the eastward where he knew was a witch's grave. He sang there spells of the dead to the Vala; of necessity she must rise—a corpse—and answer:

5. 'What man is this to me unknown, who torment adds to my toilsome way? I was snowed on with snow, and dashed with rain, I was drenched with dew, I have long been dead.'

Odin.

6. "They call me Waywanting, I am son of Warwanting; tell me tidings of Hel, I will tell of the world. For whom are the benches strewn with rings, for whom is the fair platform flooded with gold?'

Vala.

7. 'Here stands for Baldr brewed the mead, the shining cup, the shield lies over, but the Gods' Folk all are in despair. Of necessity have I spoken, now will I cease.'

Odin.

8. 'Cease not, Vala! still will I ask you, I must see yet onward till all I know: who will be the slayer of Baldr, who Odin's son will of life bereave? '

Vala.

9. 'Höd shall bear there the high-grown Fame-bough, he will be the slayer of Baldr, yes, Odin's son will of life bereave. Of necessity have I spoken, now will I cease.'

10. 'Cease not, Vala, still will I ask you, I must see yet onward till all I know: —who shall work revenge for the woe on Höd, and lay on the cremation fire Baldr's foe?

THE FORMING VERSES

Vala.
11. 'Rind shall bear Vali in the western halls; he, Odin's son, shall fight one night old. Nor hand will he wash, nor head will he comb till he lay on the cremation fire Baldr's foe. Of necessity have I spoken, now will I cease.'
Odin.
12. 'Cease not, Vala, still will I ask you, I must see yet onward till all I know: who are the maidens who weep at will, and up toward heaven their neck veils fling?'
Vala.
13. 'Not Way wanting are you as I had seen, but you are Odin, the ancient creator!'
Odin.
'No Vala are you nor woman wise, but of three giants you are mother!'
Vala.
14. 'Ride homeward, Odin, glorying in your gain! for so shall no being ever meet me more, before Loki journeys from his fetters free, and the Destroyers come at the Powers' great Doom.'

VIKINGS BÓK

NOTES

2. —*Sleipnir: Odin's eight-footed steed; see Vsp. en skamma, st. 8. Misty. Hel: The dwelling place of the Goddess Hel, daughter of Loki and Angrbotha; see Vsp. en skamma, st. 8, Ls. Introd. A hound: Garm; see Vsp. 44.*

3. —*The father of spells or magic, as in Hav. Odin sang some such song as that mentioned in Hav., st. 156.*

6. —*Waywanting: Odin as wanderer; Cf. Gangleri, Grm., st. 49.*

9. —*The Fame bough or mistletoe which, according to Snorri, Loki puts "into the hands of blind Höd; see Vsp. 32, Ls. st. 28, Fj. st. 26.*

11. —*Rind, the giant wife of Odin; see Gr., st. 6. Vali, see Vm. 57; Vsp. en skamma, st. 1.*

12. —*Their neck veils: Icelandic, halsa skautum, is of uncertain meaning. Skaut is used for sheet, corner, quarter of the heavens, sail, part of a woman's dress. Dt. inclines to the above; G., sail corners. If the expression is nautical, Wimmer suggests that the maidens are wave daughters of Aegir; see Hym.,st. 2.*

LOKI'S MOCKING
At the banquet of Aegir

Aegir, who is also called Gymir (the Binder), invited the Gods to an ale feast after he had got possession of the great cauldron—as already told. To this banquet came Odin and Frigg, his wife. Thor came not because he was journeying in the East-country, but his wife Sif was there, and Bragi, with his wife Idun; Tyr also, who was one-handed, because the wolf Fenrir had torn off the other hand while the Gods were binding him. There were Njord and his wife Skadi, Frey and his servants Barley and Beyla, Freyja, Vidar, the son of Odin, with many other Gods and Elves; there, moreover, was Loki. Aegir had two servants—Nimble-snatcher and Fire-stirrer. Shining gold was used in the hall for the light of fire, the ale bore itself, and the place was held as a Holy peace-stead. Men praised Aegir's servants, and said often how good they were; but Loki could not tolerate this, and he slew Nimble-snatcher. The Gods all shook their shields and cried out against Loki, and chased him away to the woods, and then began themselves again to drink. But Loki turned back, and finding Fire- stirrer standing without, he hailed him:

Loki.
1. Tell me, Fire-stirrer—but when you stand move not a single step—what are the sons of the war-Gods saying over the ale-cup here within?

Fire-stirrer.
2. Of their weapons are speaking the sons of the war-Gods, they boast of their battle-fame; but amid Gods and Elves who within are gathered, not one is your friend in his words.

Loki.
3. I shall now enter the halls of Aegir this banquet to behold: mockery and strife will I bring to the God's sons, and mingle sorrow with their mead.

Fire-stirrer.
4. Know, if you enter the halls of Aegir this banquet to behold, if reproach and slander on the Holy Powers you pour they shall wipe out your words upon you.

Loki.
5. Know you, Fire-stirrer, if we two must fight together with wounding words, —if you talk too freely you soon shall find me in answering ready and rich.

Then Loki entered the hall, and when those assembled saw who was come in they all became silent.

Loki.
6. Thirsty come I, the Rover of Air, to this feasting hall from afar; I would ask the Gods to give me but one sweet mouthful of the mead to drink.
7. Why all silent you sullen Gods? Can you speak no single word? Make me room on the bench, give me place at the banquet, or bid me hasten homeward hence.
Bragi.
8. Nor place at the banquet nor room on the bench the Gods shall give to you; well they know for what manner of being they should spread so fair a feast.
Loki.
9. Mind you, Odin, how we two of old like brothers mingled our blood? Then said you that never was ale-cup sweet unless it were borne to us both.
Odin.
10. Rise up, Vidar, and give the Wolf's father bench-room at the banquet, lest Loki shame us with scornful speeches here in Aegir's halls.

Then Vidar arose and poured out ale for Loki, who so greeted the Gods before he drank: —

11. Hail, you Gods, and Goddesses, hail! hail all you Holy Powers! —save only one who sits within, you, Bragi, upon the bench!
Bragi.
12. Steed and sword from my store will I give you and reward you well with rings lest you pour your hate on the gracious Powers. Rouse not their wrath against you!

THE FORMING VERSES

Loki.
13. Not steeds nor rings will you ever own as long as you live, Bragi: you are wariest in war, and shyest of shot of all Gods and Elves herein.

Bragi.
14. Were I outside now even in such mood as within the halls of Aegir, that head of yours would I hold in my hand: —it were little reward for your lie!

Loki.
15. Bold seem you sitting, but slack are you doing, Bragi, you pride of the bench! Come forth and fight if in truth you are angry; a bold warrior bides not to think.

Idun.
16. Rather Bragi, I beg for the sake of blood-kindred, and of all the war-sons of Odin, upbraid not Loki with bitter speeches here in Aegir's halls.

Loki.
17. Silence, Idun! I swear, of all women you the most wanton are; who could fling those fair-washed arms of yours about your brother's slayer.

Idun.
18. I blame you not, Loki, with bitter speeches here in Aegir's halls. I seek but to sooth the ale-stirred Bragi, lest in your fierceness you fight.

Gefjon.
19. Why, you Gods split with wounding words struggle you here in the hall? Who knows not Loki, that he loathes all beings and mocks in his madness of soul?

Loki.
20. Silence, Gefjon! I will tell that tale of him who once stole your heart, —that fair admirer who gave you a shining necklace, him you did hold in yours arms.

Odin.
21. Wild are you, Loki, and mindless now, so rousing Gefjon to wrath! I see she knows all the fate of the world even as surely as I.

Loki.
22. Silence, Odin! When could you ever rule battles of men rightly? Often have you given to them who had earned not, to the slothful victory in strife.

Odin.
23. Know, if ever I gave to them who had earned not, to the slothful victory in strife, eight winters were you below in the earth like a maiden, milking cows, and there you gave birth to children, —which I see was a woman's lot.

Loki.
24. But you in Samsey were weaving magic and making spells like a witch: you did pass as wizard through the world of men, —which I see was a woman's way.

Frigg.
25. Tell you to no man the shameful tale of the deeds you did of old, —how you two Gods wrought in ancient time; —what is gone is best forgot.

Loki.
26. Silence, Frigg! who has Earth's spouse for a husband, and has ever yearned after men! Ve the Holy, and Vili the lustful both lay in yours arms, wife of Odin.

Frigg.
27. Know, if I had but in Aegir halls, a son like my Baldr, the slain, you would never come whole through the host of the Gods but fiercely you should be assailed.

Loki.
28. Would have me, Frigg, tell a few more yet of these shameful stories of mine? It was I wrought the Woe, that hereafter you will not see Baldr ride back to the halls.

Freyja.
29. Mad are you, Loki, to tell so the shame and grim deeds wrought by you Gods! Frigg knows, I see, all the fate of the world; though she whispers of it to none.

Loki.
30. Silence, Freyja! Full well I know you and faultless are you not found; of the Gods and Elves who here are gathered each one has you made your mate.

THE FORMING VERSES

Freyja.
31. False your tongue is! Too soon it will sing its own song of woe, as I see. Angry are the Gods, and the Goddesses angry, rueful you soon shall run home.

Loki.
32. Silence, Freyja! You are a sorceress all with evil mixed: once at your brother's the happy Gods caught you, and then were you frightened, Freyja!

Njord.
33. Small harm it seems if by chance a woman both lover and husband have; but behold the horror now in the halls, the vile God who children have borne!

Loki.
34. Silence, Njord! You were eastward sent as hostage from here by the Gods; there into your mouth flowed the maids of Hymir and used you as channel for their floods.

Njord.
35. Yet was I gladdened when sent afar, as hostage from here by the Gods; there a son I got me, the foe of none, and highest held among Gods.

Loki.
36. Silence now, Njord! Set bounds to your lying; I will no longer let this be hid—with your own sister that son you got, though he is not worse than one supposed.

Tyr.
37. No! Frey is the best of all bold riders who enter the courtyard of the Gods; nor wife nor maiden he makes to weep, but he breaks the prisoner's bonds.

Loki.
38. Silence, Tyr! Who in truth could never bring good will between two; the tale will I tell of that right hand which Fenrir robbed from you once.

Tyr.
39. If I want for a hand for your Wolf-son, you; we both bear burden of want: and it is ill with the Wolf who must wait in bonds till the twilight come of the Powers.

Loki.
40. Be silent, Tyr, while I tell of the son whom your wife got once by me: not even a penny or arms length of cloth did you get for your wrong, poor wretch!
Frey.
41. I see Fenrir lying at the mouth of the flood; he shall wait till the Powers perish; and you, mischief-maker, shall meet with like fate if you hold not here your peace.
Loki.
42. Wealth gave you, Frey, for Gymir's maid, you did sell your sword for Gerd; but how shall you fight when the sons of fire through the Murk-wood ride, poor wretch?
Barley.
43. Were I of Ing's Folk even as Frey—owned I a land blest as Elfhome—I would crush like marrow that croaker of ill, and break all his bones into bits.
Loki.
44. What is that wee thing whining and fawning, snuffling and snapping, I see? Ever at Frey's ear, flattering and chattering, or murmuring under the mill!
Barley.
45. Barley, I am named, too bold and brisk I am called by Gods and men! Here am I glorying that Odin's sons all are drinking ale together!
Loki.
46. Silence, Barley-corn! Never could you even serve meat among men: and when they fought you could scarce be found, safe beneath the bed-straw hiding.
Heimdal.
47. So drunk are you, Loki, you have lost your wits; why will you not cease from your scoffing? Ale beyond measure so masters man that he keeps no watch on his words.
Loki.
48. Silence, Heimdal! That hard life of yours was settled for you long since: with weary back must you ever bide, and keep watch, you warder of Gods!

THE FORMING VERSES

Skadi.
49. Unthinking are you, Loki, but brief while shall you with free tail frolic so: before long the Gods shall bind you with guts of your ice-cold son to a sword.
Loki.
50. If in truth the Gods shall bind me with guts of my ice-cold son to a rock, know that first and last was I found at the death when we set upon Thiaxi, your sire.
Skadi.
51. If first and last you were found at the death when you set upon Thiazi, my sire, know that in house or home of my shall be shown you little love!
Loki.
52. Milder were your words to Loki once when you told him come to your bed; for such tales, I see, will be told of us two, if we own all our acts of shame.

Then Sif came forth, and poured out mead for Loki in the foaming cup.

Sif.
53. Hail now, Loki! drink this frosty cup filled with the old mead full. At least grant that I, of the kindred of Gods alone am free from all fault.

Loki took the horn and drank:

54. You alone were blameless had you in bearing been sly and shrewish with men; but Thor's wife had one lover at least, as I know, even Loki the wily-wise.
Beyla.
55. All the fells are quaking, fast is the Thunderer faring, I believe, from home! He will soon bring to silence him who so slanders all beings here in the hall.
Loki.
56. Silence, Beyla, wife of Barley-corn all with foulness filled! Never amid the Gods came one so uncouth, you bond-maid stained and soiled.

Then came the Thunderer in, and spoke: —

57. Silence, vile being! My hammer of might, Mjöllnir, shall spoil you of speech. I will strike that rock-head from off your shoulders, and soon will your life-days be spent.
Loki.
58. It is the Son of Earth who enters the hall! Why do you threaten so, Thor? Never will you venture to fight with the Wolf; he shall swallow the War-father whole.
Thor.
59. Silence, vile being! My hammer of might, Mjöllnir, shall spoil you of speech. I will drive you forth to the eastern land and no man shall see you more.
Loki.
60. Of your eastern journeys never should you tell unto men the tale; how once in a glove-thumb you, warrior, did crouch, and scarce could think yourself Thor.
Thor.
61. Silence, vile being! My hammer of might, Mjöllnir, shall spoil you of speech; this right hand shall smite you with Hrungnir's slayer, till each bone of you shall be broke.
Loki.
62. Though by chance you threaten with your hammer of might, long will my life be, I see; sharp were Skrymir's thongs, mind you, when starving you could not get at the food?
Thor.
63. Silence, vile being! My hammer of might, Mjöllnir, shall spoil you of speech. With Hrungnir's slayer I will smite you to Hel, down beneath the gates of the dead.
Loki.
64. Before sons and daughters of Gods have I spoken, even as I was moved by my mind: now at length I go, and for you alone, for well, I see, you will fight.
65. You have brewed your ale, but such banquet, Aegir, never more shall you make. May flames play high over your wealth in the hall and scorch the skin of your back!

THE FORMING VERSES

Then Loki went forth and hid himself in Franang's stream in the form of a salmon, where the Gods caught him and bound him with the guts of his son Narfi. But his other son Vali was turned into a wolf. Skadi took a poisonous snake and fastened it up over Loki, so that poison dripped from it upon his face. Sigyn, his wife, sat by, and held a basin under the drops. And when the basin was full she cast the poison away, but meanwhile the drops fell upon Loki, and he struggled so fiercely against it that the whole earth shook with his strivings, which are now called earthquakes.

NOTES

As already told. See Hm. East-country, or Jötunheim.
8. —Bragi, the God of poetry.
9. —The mingling of blood sealed a brotherhood in arms. Loki, Odin, and Hoenir were companions in many strange adventures.
10. —Vidar, see Grm. 17; Vsp., st. 54. Loki was the father of Fenrir, see st. 39; Vsp. en skamma, st. 8.
16. —Idun, Bragi's wife. The myth of st. 17 is unknown.
20. —Gefjon is only mentioned here in the Poetical Edda. The myth is usually told of Freya; see Thrk st. 12 and [Bray's] Intro.
23. —This strophe perhaps alludes to another version of the myth of Vsp. en skamma, st. 9.
24. —Samsey, modern Samsu, north of Funen.
26, line i. —This line has often been misunderstood, by Snorri and later critics. The literal, you are Fjorgynn's maid, has been rendered, you are Fjorgynn's daughter. But Fjorgynn is only another name for Odin in his character as the husband of Fjbrgyn or Jord, the Earth, and mother of Thor. Ve and Vili, the brothers of Odin, may also be taken as different aspects of the same God. The name used in the text for Odin is Vidrir, the Stormer; see Grm., st. 51.
28. —The only allusion in the Poetical Edda to Loki's share in the death of Baldr; see Bdr. [Bray's] Intro. Possibly it only refers to Loki's refusal to weep (Nd. Dalt., 41).

29. —*By you Gods: so Gering and Dt. HI. take vthra.*

32. —*No such myth of Frey or Freyja is mentioned elsewhere.*

34. —*Njord figures here in his character of Sea-God; see Fragments from Su. E*

36. —*A son, presumably had with the giantess Skadi, but in Ynglinga Saga it is stated that Njord was married to his sister, and had a son and daughter, Frey and Freyja, before even he was sent as hostage by the Wanes to the Aesir.*

38. —*See [Bray's] Intro.*

39. —*Twilight of the Powers or Ragna rokr: This is the only use of rokr in the poems, which has given rise to the phrase "twilight of the Gods." The more usual form was rok or fate.*

40. —*A lost myth.*

41. —*The flood, called Vamm or Van by Snorri, is a river of Hel proceeding from the moisture which flowed out of Fenrir's jaws while the great Wolf lay bound in torture.*

42. —*Frey is slain by Surt, the Fire-giant, at the Doom of the Gods; see Vsp. 54. Gymir, Gerd, see Skm.*

43. —*Ing was the half divine ancestor of the Germanic Folk who gave his name to the Ynglings or Swedes (Hdl., st. 11) and to the Ingvines mentioned by Tacitus. In Sweden he became associated with Frey, who was there the chief God. Elf-home, see Grm., st. 5.*

49. —*A sword: we are told by Snorri that Loki is bound to three sharp stones.*

50. —*Thiazi was slain by Thor; see Hrbl., st. 19; Vsp. en skamma, st. 3.*

52. —*Another lost myth.*

53. —*Sif, Thor's wife; see [Bray's] Intro. to Gm. Hrbl., st. 48.*

THE WISE WOMAN'S SHORTER PROPHECY

1. Eleven only the war Gods numbered when Baldr sank on the cremation fire down; but Vali showed him strong to avenge it and slew before long his brother's slayer.
2. Father of Baldr was Odin, Bur's son.
    *   *   *   *   *   *   *   *   *   *
3. Frey wedded Gerd; she was Gymir's daughter, and Aurboda's of Jötun Folk; Thiazi also came of their kindred, the shape-shifting giant, Skadi's sire.
4. Much have I told you, yet more I remember; by necessity must one know it so, —will you know further?
5. Witch and Horse-thief are sprung from Frost-bringer,
6. All the Valas sprung from Forest-wolf, all the wizards sprung from Wish-giver, all the sorcerers sprung from Swart-head; and all the Jötuns come from Ymir.
7. Much have I told you, yet more I remember; by necessity must one know it so, —will you know further?
8. Woe-bringer bore the wolf to Loki, with Swadilfari begat he Sleipnir. But one was deemed the deadliest of all,—the monster brood from Loki born.
9. When the heart of a woman—home of love—he ate half-burned with linden wood, and bore before long a loathly being from where witches all in the world are sprung.
10. Much have I told you, yet more I remember, by necessity must one know it so, —will you know further?
11. One was there born in days of old, bounded with great power, of the kindred of Gods. Nine giant maidens bore that being armed with glory on the rim of earth.
12. Yelper bore him, Griper bore him, Foamer bore him, Sand-strewer bore him, She-wolf bore him, Sorrow-whelmer, Dusk and Fury and Ironsword.
13. He was bound with all the power of Earth, of the ice-cold sea, and of sacred swine-blood.
14. He was the One born greater than any; bound with all the power of Earth. Men call him ever the richest ruler, Rig, the kinsman of every Folk.

15. Much have I told you, yet more I remember, by necessity must one know it so, —will you know further?
16. The sea shall rise in storms to heaven, it shall sweep over the land and the skies shall yield in showers of snow and biting blasts at the Doom of the Powers, the Gods of war.
17. There shall come hereafter another mightier whose name I dare not now make known: few there are who may see beyond when Odin fares to fight with the Wolf.

NOTES

Vala or Witch, see Bdr, st. 4.
1. —Vali, see Bdr., st. 11 ; Vm., st. 51.
2.—Bur means son, e.g. of Buri, the first-born of the God's Folk, and according to Snorri, the grandfather of Odin ; see Vsp. st. 4 and Introd. to Vm.
3.—Gerd, see Skm. Aur-boda, or Moisture-bringer? Thiazi took the form of an eagle; see Ls. st. 50, Introd., and Hrbl. st. 19.
6.—Ymir, see Vm. st. 21.
8.—Woe-bringer, or Angrbotha, a giantess, who was the mother of Fenrir, the World Serpent and Hel (Sn. E.). Sleipnir, see Bdr., st. 2.
9.—This strophe is perhaps explained by Vsp. st. 21, when the Gods burn Golden-draught, the witch who is ever born anew.
11-14.—No name is mentioned in the text, but these strophes clearly refer to Heimdal or Rig ; see [Bray's] Intro., Vsp. st. 7, and Rth.
17.—Another mightier probably anticipates the coming of Christianity. [The present editor believes that this passage may have nothing to do with monotheism.]

THE WISE WOMAN'S PROPHECY

1. Hearing I ask all Holy Kindreds, high and low-born, sons of Heimdal! You too, Odin, who bids me utter the oldest tidings of men that I remember!

(The World's beginning.)

2. I remember of old were born the Jötuns, they who in times past fostered me: nine worlds I remember, nine in the Tree, the glorious Fate Tree that springs beneath the Earth.

3. It was the earliest of times when Ymir lived; then was sand nor sea nor cooling wave, nor was Earth found ever, nor Heaven on high, there was Yawning Chasm and nowhere grass:

4. before the sons of the God had uplifted the world-plain, and fashioned Middle Earth, the glorious Earth. Sun shone from the south, on the world's bare stones—then was Earth overgrown with herbage of green.

5. Sun, Moon's companion, out of the south her right hand flung round the rim of heaven. Sun knew not yet where she had her hall; nor knew the stars where they had their place; nor ever the Moon what might he owned.

(Ordering of Times and Seasons.)

6. Then went all the Powers to their thrones of doom—the most Holy Gods—and over this took counsel: to Night and the New-Moons names they gave: they named the Morning, and named the Mid-day, Afternoon, Evening, —to count the years.

(The Golden Age till the coming of Fate.)

7. Gathered the Gods on the Eternal Plains; they set on high their courts and temples; they founded forges, wrought rich treasures, tongs they hammered and fashioned tools.

8. They played at tables in court and were joyous, —little they wanted for wealth of gold. —Until there came forth three of the giant Folk, all fearful maidens, from Jötunheim.

(Creation of the Dwarfs.)

9. Then went all the Powers to their thrones of doom, the most Holy Gods, —and over this took counsel: whom should they make the lord of dwarfs out of Ymir's blood, and his dark limbs.

10. Mead-drinker then was made the highest, but Durin second of all the dwarfs; and out of the earth these two-shaped beings in form like man, as Durin sought.

11. New Moon, Waning-moon, All-thief, Dallier, North and South and East and West. Corpse-like, Death-like, Niping, Dainn, Bifur, Bafur, Bömbur, Nori, Ann and Onar, Ai, Mead-wolf.

12. Vigg and Wand-elf, Wind-elf, Thrainn, Thekk and Thorin, Thror, Vit, and Lit, Nyr and Regin, New-counsel, Wise-counsel, —now have I numbered the dwarfs rightly.

13. Fili, Kili, Fundin, Nali, Heptifili, Hannar, Sviur, Frar, Hornbori, Fraeg and Loni, Aurvang, Jari, Oaken-shield.

14. It is time to number in Dallier's song-mead all the dwarf-kind of Lofar's Folk, —who from earth's threshold, the Plains of Moisture, sought below the Sandy-realms.

15. There were Draupnir and Dolgthrasir, Har and Haugspori, Hlevang, Gloin, Dori, Ori, Duf, Andvari, Skirfir, Virfir, Skafid, Ai.

16. Elf and Yngvi, Oaken-shield, Fjalar and Frost, Fin and Ginar. So shall be told throughout all time the line who were born of Lofar's Folk.

(Creation of Man and Woman.)

17. Then came three Gods of the Aesir kindred, mighty and blessed, towards their home. They found on the seashore, wanting power, with fate unwoven, an Ash and Elm.

18. Spirit they had not, and mind they owned not, —blood, nor voice nor fair appearance. Spirit gave Odin, and mind gave Hönir, blood gave Lodur, and aspect fair.

THE FORMING VERSES

(The Tree of Life.)

19. An ash I know standing, it is called Yggdrasil, a high tree sprinkled with shining drops; come dews there from which fall in the dales; it stands ever green over the well of Wyrd.

20. There are the Maidens, all things knowing, three in the hall which stands beneath the Tree. One is named 'Wyrd,' the second 'Being'—who grave on tablets—but 'Shall' the third. They lay down laws, they choose out life, they speak the doom of the sons of men.

(The War of the Gods.)

21. I remember the first great war in the world, when Goldendraught they pierced with spears, and burned in the hall of Odin the High One; thrice they burned her, the three times born, —often, not seldom—yet still she lives.

22. Men called her 'Witch,' when she came to their dwellings, flattering seeress; wands she enchanted, spells many wove she, light-hearted wove them, and of evil women was ever the joy.

23. Then went all the Powers to their thrones of doom, the most Holy Gods, and over this took counsel: whether the Aesir should pay a were-gild or all Powers together make peaceful offering.

24. But Odin hurled and shot amid the host; and still raged the first great war in the world. Broken then were the bulwarks of Asgard, the Wanes, war wary, trampled the field.

(War with the Jötuns.)

25. Then went all the Powers to their thrones of doom, the most Holy Gods, and over this took counsel: who all the air had mingled with poison and Freyja had yielded to the Folk of Jötuns.

26. Alone fought the Thunderer with raging heart—seldom he rests when he hears such tidings. Oaths were broken, words and swearing, all solemn treaties made between them.

(The Secret Pledges of the Gods.)

27. I know where Heimdal's hearing is hidden under the heaven-bright Holy Tree, which I see ever showered with falling streams from All-father's pledge. —Would you know further, and what?

28. I sat alone enchanting when came the Dread One, the ancient God, and gazed in my eyes: 'What do you ask of me? why do you prove me?'

29. All know I, Odin, —yes, where you have hidden your eye in the wondrous well of Mimir, who each morn from the pledge of All-father drinks the mead—Would you know further, and what?

30. Then Odin bestowed on me rings and trinkets for magic spells and the wisdom of wands. I saw far and wide into every world.

31. From far I saw the Valkyries coming ready to ride to the Gods' Folk. Fate held a shield, and Lofty followed War and Battle, Bond and Spearpoint. Numbered now are the Warfather's maidens, Valkyries, ready to ride over Earth.

32. I saw for Baldr, the bleeding God, the child of Odin, his doom concealed. High over the fields, there stood upgrown, most slender and fair, the mistletoe.

33. And there came from that plant, though slender it seemed, the harm flung missile which Höd did shoot. But Baldr's brother was born before long; that son of Odin fought one night old;

34. for never hand he bathed, nor head, before he laid on the bale-fire Baldr's foe. But Frigg long wept over the woe of Valhöll in Fen's moist halls—Would you know further, and what?

(Vision into Hel and Jötunheim.)

35. I saw lying bound in Cauldron-grove one like the form of guile-loving Loki. And there sat Sigyn, yet over her husband rejoicing little. —Would you know further, and what?

36. From the eastward a flood, the Stream of Fear, bore swords and daggers through Poison-dales. ...

THE FORMING VERSES

37. To the northward stood on the Moonless Plains, the golden hall of the Sparkler's kin; and a second stood in the Uncooled realm, a feast-hall of Jötuns, 'Fire' it is called:

38. And far from the sun I saw a third on the Strand of Corpses, with doors set northward: down through the roof dripped poison-drops, for that hall was woven with serpents' backs.

39. I saw there wading the overwhelming streams wolf-like murderers, men forsworn, and those who another's love-whisperer had wiled. The dragon, Fierce-stinger, fed on corpses, a wolf tore men. —Would you know further, and what?

40. Far east in Iron-wood sat an old giantess, Fenrir's offspring she fostered there. From among them all does one come forth, in guise of a troll, to snatch the sun.

41. He is gorged, as on lives of dying men; he reddens the place of the Powers like blood. Malignant grows the sunshine of summer after, all baleful the storms. —Would you know further, and what?

(Signs of Doom.)

42. Sits on a mound and strikes his harp the gleeful Swordsman, warder of giant-wives; over him crows in the roosting tree the fair red cock who Fjalar is called.

43. Crows over the Gods the Golden-combed; he wakes the heroes in War-father's dwellings; and crows yet another beneath the earth, a dark red rooster in the halls of Hel.

44. Loud bays Garm before Gaping-Hel; the bond shall be broken the Wolf run free. Hidden things I know; still onward I see the great Doom of the Powers, the Gods of war.

45. Brothers shall fight and be as murderers; sisters' children shall stain their kinship. It is ill with the world; comes fearful whoredom, a Sword age, Axe age, —shields are split, a Wind age, Wolf age, before the world sinks. Never shall man then spare another.

46. Mim's sons arise; the Fate Tree kindles at the roaring sound of Gjalla-horn. Loud blows Heimdal, the horn is aloft, and Odin speaks with Mimir's head.

47. Groans the Ancient Tree, Fenrir is freed, shivers, yet standing, Yggdrasil's ash.
48. How do the Gods fare, how do the Elves fare? All Jötunheim rumbles, the Gods are in council; before the stone doors the dwarfs are groaning, a rock-wall finding—Would you know further, and what?
49. Loud bays Garm before Gaping-hel: the bond shall be broken, the Wolf run free. Hidden things I know; still onward I see the great Doom of the Powers, the Gods of war.

(Gathering of the Destroyers.)

50. Drives Hrym from the East holding shield on high; the World-serpent thrashes in Jötun-rage; he lashes the waves; screams a pale-beaked eagle, rending corpses, the Death boat is launched.
51. Sails the boat from the East; Muspel's sons over the sea are coming, and Loki steering, brother of Byleist, he fares on the way with Fenrir and all the monster kinsmen.
52. Rides Surt from the South fire, curse of branches, sun of the war Gods, gleams from his sword. The rock-hills crash, the troll-wives totter, souls flock Helward, and heaven is split.

(The last battles of the Gods.)

53. Soon comes to pass Frigg's second woe, when Odin fares to fight with the wolf; then must he fall, her lord beloved, and Beli's bright slayer must bow before Surt.
54. Comes forth the stalwart son of the War-father, Vidar, to struggle with the deadly beast; lets he the sword from his right hand leap into Fenrir's heart, and avenged is the father.
55. Comes forth the glorious offspring of Earth, Thor, to struggle with the glistening Serpent.
56. Strikes in his wrath the Warder of Midgard, while mortals all their homes forsake; nine feet recoils he, the son of Odin, bowed, from the dragon who fears not shame.

THE FORMING VERSES

(The End of the World.)

57. The sun is darkened, Earth sinks in the sea, from heaven turn the bright stars away. Rages smoke with fire, the life-feeder, high flame plays against heaven itself.

58. Loud howls Garm before Gaping-hel, the bond shall be broken, the Wolf run free; hidden things I know; still onward I see the great Doom of the Powers, the Gods of war.

(The new World.)

59. I see rising up a second time earth from the ocean, green anew; the waters fall, on high the eagle flies over the fell and catches fish.

60. The Gods are gathered on the Eternal Plains; they speak concerning the great World Serpent, and remember there things of former fame and the Mightiest God's old mysteries.

61. Then shall be found the wondrous-seeming golden tables hid in the grass, those they had used in days of old.

62. And there unsown shall the fields bring forth; all harm shall be healed; Baldr will come—Höd and Baldr shall dwell in Valhöll, at peace the war Gods. —Would you know further, and what?

63. Then Hönir shall cast the twigs of divining, and the sons shall dwell of Odin's brothers in Wind-home wide. —Would you know further, and what?

64. I see yet a hall more fair than the sun, roofed with gold in the Fire-sheltered realm; ever shall dwell there all Holy Beings, blest with joy through the days of time.

(Coming of the new Power, passing of the old.)

65. Comes from on high to the great Assembly the Mighty Ruler who orders all.

66. Fares from beneath a dim dragon flying, a glistening snake from the Moonless Fells. Fierce-stinger bears the dead on his pinions away over the plains. I sink now and cease.

VIKINGS BÓK

NOTES

1. —Sons of Heimdal or Rig, hence men are called Holy; see Rth.
2. —Nine worlds; see Vm.,st,43. Fate Tree, Yggdrasil; see st. 19; Grm., st. 31; Hav., st. 137; Fj., st. 14.
3. —Ymir; see Vm., st. 21, 29.
4. —The sons of the God, or sons of Bur; see Vsp. en skamma, st. 2.
6. —Thrones of doom, beneath Yggdrasil; see Grm., st. 30.
8 —All-fearful maidens: Cf. this stanza with 60, 61; the Norns, st. 20.
9. —Ymir is here called Brimir.
11-16. —A translation of these obscure names has only been given where it seems to suggest the character of the dwarfs.
14. —Dallier's song-mead is so taken by Dt. and Hl. as a synonym for poetry; cf. Snorri's "Dallier's drink." Dallier is a dwarf well known in the Edda, and is chosen to represent his Folk who brewed the mead (Sn.E.). This dwarf migration from the earth's surface is also suggested by Dt, and Hl.
17. —Elm: the meaning of Icelandic embla is doubtful.
18. —Hönir: a God of wisdom. Lodur probably stands for Loki, for these three were always companions.
20. —Wyrd, see Gg., st. 7.
21. —The story of this war between the Aesir amd Wanes is never fully told, but is the subject of constant allusions; see Vm., 39. Golden draught, see V'sp. en skamma, st. 9.
22. —Witch, of Vala.
23. —Lines 2 and 3 are so understood by Hl.
25. —For Snorri's account, see [Bray's] Intro. Freyja is here called the bride of Ud or Ottar; see Hdl
28. —Heimdal's hearing was celebrated. Dt. and Hl. so correct the hitherto accepted translation horn of Icl. hljöþ.
29. —Mimir, a water giant. He is the wise teacher and counsellor of the Gods, although a Jötun; see Hav., st. 139.
32. 34. —See Bdr,, st. 8-12.
34. —Fen's moist halls: the home of Frigg.
35. —Set Ls. prose ending.
37. —The Sparkler: a dwarf and forger of the Gods' treasures; see Grm., st. 43.

THE FORMING VERSES

39. Fierce-stinger, see Grm., st. 35. 40. Ironwood: a famous mythical forest in Jötunheim. Fenrir's offspring: Skoll, who pursued the sun, and Hati, who followed the moon; see Grm., st. 39.

42 —The gleeful Swordsman is the warder of Jötunheim, and corresponds with Heimdal, the watchman of the Gods.

43. —The Golden-combed, see Fj., st. 17.

44.—Garm, the Hel hound; see Bdr., st. 2. He and Tyr fight and slay one another (Sn.E.). Gaping-hel, Icelandic Gnipa-hel, is descriptive of the craggy rock entrance which forms the mouth of Hel. The Wolf, see Ls. 39.

46.—Mini or Mimir: his sons must be the waters of the well, or the streams that flow from it. Compare Aegir and Hymir's daughters; Hym. st. 2, Ls. st. 34. The story of Mimir's head is told in Ynglinga S. (see [Bray's] Intro.), but here an earlier form of the myth is implied, in which the head is a well-spring of wisdom. The Fate Tree: the unemended mjötutþ of the manuscript has suggested various renderings—the judge appears; fate approaches.

47. —Fenrir, not Loki, must be intended by Jötun of the text, for Loki was always reckoned among the Gods.

50. —Hrym, the leader of the Frost-giants. A pale-beaked eagle, Corpse-swallower; see Vm. 37. Death-boat or Naglfar, the Nail-ferry, said by Snorri to be made of the nails of dead men.

51.—Byleist is unknown except as Loki's brother.

52 —Surt, see Vm., st. 53.

53.—Beli's bright slayer, or Frey. Beli, Snorri tells us, was a giant whom Frey slew with a stag's horn for lack of the sword which he had given for Gerd; see Skm. st. 16, Ls. st. 42.

55. —The Serpent, see Hym., st. 23.

62. —Valhöll, called here the victory halls of Hropt (Odin).

63.—The twigs, set Hym., st. 1.

64.—Fire-sheltered realm, Icelandic (Gimle from gim, fire, and hl'e, shelter; Dt. and Hl.), which has often been translated jeweled; but the above meaning shows this hall in contrast to the others of st. 37 and 38.

TRANSLATORS INDEX

Aegir; a sea giant.
Aesir; the line of Gods, distinguished from Wanes.
Agnar; brother of Geirrod, son of Geirrod.
Ai; name of two dwarfs.
Alf; kinsman of Ottar.
Alf the Old; son of Dag and Thora, grandfather of Ottar.
Ali; kinsman of Ottar.
All-father; Odin.
All-fleet; a horse.
All-green; an island.
All-thief; a dwarf.
All-wielder; a giant, father of Thiazi.
All-wise; (Aliss) a dwarf, a Jötun.
Almveig; wife of Halfdan.
Am; son of Dag and Thora.
Andvari; a dwarf.
Angantyr; Ottar's rival, a berserk.
Ann; a dwarf.
Arngrim; father of twelve berserks.
Asgard; dwelling of the Aesir or Gods.
Ash; the first man.
Athlings; a mythical Folk.
Atvard; one of the builders of Menglöd's hall.
Aud; mother of Harald Wartooth.
Aurboda; mother of Gerd.
Anrvang; a dwarf.
Babe; son of Earl.
Baldr; the God, son of Odin.
Bale-thorn; a giant, grandfather of Odin.
Bale-worker; Odin.
Bari; a builder of Menglöd's hall.
Barley; Frey's servant.

THE FORMING VERSES

Barri; a berserk.
Bashful; daughter of Churl.
Bath-tubs; two rivers.
Battle; (Hildr) a Valkyrie.
Battle-wolf; a ferryman.
Being; one of the Norns.
Beli; a giant slain by Frey.
Bergelm; forefather of all Jötuns.
Bestla; a giantess, mother of Odin.
Cauldron-grove; Loki's prison.
Child; son of Earl.
Chosen Warriors; heroes of the battle field bidden to Valhöll by Odin.
Churl; son of Rig and Grandmother, father of all freeborn peasants.
Clay-giant; Ymir.
Cloggy; daughter of Thrall.
Cooler; shelterer from the sun.
Corpse-like; a dwarf.
Corpse-swallower; a giant eagle, maker of the wind.
Counsel-fierce; a Valkyrie.
Counsel-isle-sound; home of Battle-wolf.
Counsellor; Odin.
Cow-herd; son of Thrall.
Crane-shanked maid; daughter of Thrall.
Dag; a chieftain of Halfdan's Folk.
Dain; a buck, an Elf or dwarf.
Dallier; a dwarf, a buck.
Dame; daughter of Churl.
Damp; a chieftain.
Dan; a chieftain.
Daughter-in-law; wife of Churl.
Dawning, Dawn; father of Day.
Day; personification of Day.

Day-spring; Menglöd's lover.
Dazzler of Hel; Odin.
Dead's Way; road to Valhöll.
Death-barrier; the gate of Valhöll.
Death-father; Odin.
Death-like; a dwarf.
Delling; a builder of Menglöd's hall, probably the same being as Dawning.
Descendent; son of Earl.
Dolgthrasir; a dwarf.
Doom of the Gods; Ragnarok.
Dori; a dwarf?
Draupnir; a dwarf.
Dread One; Odin.
Duf; a dwarf.
Duneyr; a buck.
Durin; a dwarf.
Dusk; one of Heimdal's mothers.
Dvalin; Dallier, a buck.
Dwarfs; [Wise, crafty beings, or Elves; of earth or rocks.]
Dyrathror; a buck.
Eager in War; Odin.
Eagle-nose; daughter of Thrall.
Earl; son of Rig and Mother.
Early-woke; a horse.
Earna; wife of Earl.
Earth; a Goddess, wife of Odin and mother of Thor.
East; a dwarf.
Eastern land; the East, Jötunheim, giant-land.
Egil; a giant, father of Thjalfi.
Elf; a dwarf.
Elf-beam; Elf-light, the sun.
Elf-home; Prey's dwelling.
Elm; the first woman.

THE FORMING VERSES

Elves; [Hidden Divine Folk; light Elves, dark Elves.]
Ember; Menglöd's hall.
Equal-ranked; Odin.
Eyfora; wife of Arngrim.
Eylimi; a hero of the Athling Folk.
Eymund; a chieftain, Halfdan's ally.
Fafnir; a dragon slain by Sigurd.
Falling-brook; home of Odin and Saga
Fame-bough; the mistletoe shot by Höd.
Farmer; son of Churl.
Fate; a Valkyrie.
Fate-tree; Yggdrasil.
Father; a nobleman.
Father of Beings; Odin.
Father of Hosts; Odin.
Father of Men; Odin.
Father of Spells; Odin.
Father of Wrath; Thor.
Fear; a river.
Fenrir; the great Wolf, son of Loki.
Fen's Moist halls; Frigg's home.
Fickle; Odin.
Fields of Labour; first home of the Gods.
Fierce-cold; grandfather of Dayspring.
Fierce-stinger; the dragon who gnaws the roots of Yggdrasil.
Fili a dwarf.
Fin; a dwarf.
Fine-flanked-steed; grandsire of Gna's horse, Hoof-flinger.
Fire; feasting hall of the Jötuns.
Fire-Giants; [Primal fire beings, enemies of the Gods.]
Fire-sheltered-realm; abode of the good after Ragnarok.
Fire-stirrer; Aegir's serving-man.

Fjalar; a giant who hoodwinked Thor, called by Snorri Utgard-loki.
Fjalar; a cock, a dwarf.
Flaming-eyed; Odin.
Flashing-eyed; Odin.
Foamer; one of Heimdal's mothers.
Folk-field; home of Freyja.
Folk-stirrer; a dwarf.
Forest-wolf; forefather of all Valas.
Forseti; a God [of justice and reconciliation. "The Presiding One." Son of Baldr and Nanna.]
Fradmar; son of Dag.
Franang's-stream; where Loki hid in the form of a salmon.
Fraeg; a dwarf.
Frar; a dwarf.
Freight-wafter; Odin.
Frey; a God, son of Njord. (See Njord, son of).
Freyja; a Goddess, daughter of Njord.
Friaut; Ottar's grandmother.
Frigg; a Goddess, wife of Odin.
Frodi; a hero of Ottar's line, Ottar's grandfather.
Frost; a dwarf.
Frost-bringer; a Frost-giant (?), father of Witch and Horsehasten.
Frost-giants; [Primal ice beings, enemies of the Gods.]
Frosty-mane; a horse of Night.
Fulla; Frigg's handmaiden.
Fundin; a dwarf.
Fury; one of Heimdal's mothers.
Gaping-hel; the rock-entrance of Hel.
Garm; the watch-dog of Hel.
Gaudy; daughter of Churl.
Gay; daughter of Churl.

THE FORMING VERSES

Gefjon; a Goddess.
Geirrod; a Jötun, King of the Goths.
Generous; one of Menglöd's handmaidens.
Gentle; one of Menglöd's handmaidens.
Gerd; a giant maiden, daughter of Gymir, wooed by Frey.
Ginar; a dwarf.
Girdle (the); the World-serpent.
Gjallahorn; Heimdals horn.
Gjuki; King of the Goths.
Glad-home; Odin's dwelling.
Glad-one; a horse.
Gleamer; a horse.
Glistener (Glasir); a grove in front of Valhöll.
Glitnir; Forseti's mansion.
Gloin; a dwarf.
Glutton; a watch-dog of Menglöd's hall.
Gna; a Goddess.
Goin; a serpent.
Golden-bristle; Freyja's boar.
Golden-comb; a cock.
Golden-draught; a Vala.
Gold-lock; a horse.
Goldy; a horse.
Grand-father; a free-born peasant.
Grand-mother; mother of Churl.
Grave-haunting worm; a serpent.
Grave-monster; a serpent.
Great-grand-father; a thrall.
Great-grand-mother; mother of Thrall.
Greed; a watch-dog of Menglöd's hall, one of Odin's wolves, n.
Grey-back; a serpent.
Grey-beard; Odin.

Gridar; a giantess.
Grimnir; Odin.
Grim Strongminded; a berserk.
Griper; one of Heimdals mothers.
Gripper; one of Geirrod's daughters.
Groa; the dead mother of Dayspring.
Guarding-warriors; one of Menglöd's handmaidens.
Gudrun; daughter of Gjuki and wife of Sigurd the Volsung.
Guest-crusher; rocky barrier in front of Menglöd's hall.
Gunnar Battle-wall; a berserk.
Gunnar, son of Gjuki; brother of Gudrun.
Gunnlod, a giantess; guardian of the Mead.
Gymir; Aegir, a frost-giant, father of Gerd.
Gyrd; son of Dag.
Guthorm Battle-snake; step-son of Gjuki.
Habrok; a hawk.
Haddings; two berserks.
Hafur; a dwarf.
Haki; son of Hvedna.
Halfdan; a king, of the Skjoldung folk.
Hannar; a dwarf.
Har; a dwarf.
Harald War-tooth; King of Denmark.
Haugspori; a dwarf.
Heaven-hill; Heimdall's home.
Hedge-breaker; a horse.
Heimdall; watchman of the Gods.
Heir; son of Earl.
Hel; the Goddess, the home of the dead.
Helm-bearer; Odin.
Heptifili; a dwarf.
Hermod; a warrior, given sword and armor by Odin.
Hero; son of Churl.

THE FORMING VERSES

Hervard; a berserk.
High One (the); Odin.
Hildigun; Ottar's great-grandmother.
Hill of Healing; the mountain on which Menglöd sat.
Hjordis; a lady of the Hraudung Folk.
Hjorvard; a berserk.
Hlebard; a giant.
Hledis; a priestess, mother of Ottar.
Hlevang; a dwarf.
Höd; a God, slayer of Baldr.
Hoenir; an Aesir God. [One of humanities creators.]
Hogni; son of Gjuki, brother of Gudrun.
Home of Strength; Thor's dwelling.
Hoodwinker; Odin.
Hoof-flinger; Gna's horse.
Hornbori; a dwarf.
Horse-thief; a giant, son of Frostbringer.
Horvi; a warrior in the train of Hrolf the Old.
Hrani; a berserk.
Hraudung; a king, father of Agnar and Geirrod.
Hraudungs; a Folk.
Hrist; a Valkyrie.
Hroerik; a king, father of Harald War-tooth.
Hrolf the Old; a chieftain.
Hrungnir; a giant slain by Thor.
Hrym; one of the giant destroyers at Ragnarok.
Hugin; a raven.
Hvedna; daughter of Hjovard.
Hymir; a frost-giant.
Hyndla; a giantess.
Idun; a Goddess, wife of Bragi.
Ifing; the river between the realms of giants and Gods.
Ing; a mythical Folk founder.
Inheritor; son of Earl.

Innstein; father of Ottar.
Iri; a builder of Menglöd's hall.
Ironsword; one of Heimdal's mothers.
Iron-wood; a forest in Jötunheim.
Isolf; a hero of Ottar's line.
Jalk; Odin.
Jörmunrek; King of the Goths.
Josurmar; son of Dag.
Jötuns; [Primeval ice or fire giants.]
Kari; a warrior of Ottar's line.
Keeler; Odin.
Ketil; great grandfather of Ottar.
King; the most famous of Earl's sons.
Kinsman; son of Earl.
Klyp; great grandfather of Ottar.
Kon; King.
Kormt; a river.
Lady; daughter of Churl.
Land of Men; [Midgard, earth?]
Land of the Slain; the battlefield.
Laufey; Loki's mother.
Leggy; son of Thrall.
Lewd; son of Thrall.
Lidskjalf; a builder of Menglöd's hall.
Life, Life-craver; the new beings born after Ragnarok.
Light-foot; a horse.
Lightning-abode; Thor's hall, n.
Lit; a dwarf.
Lodur; a God.
Lofar; a dwarf.
Lofty; a Valkyrie.
Loggy; daughter of Thrall.
Loki; an [opposing] God, father of Fenrir, Hel and the World-serpent.

THE FORMING VERSES

Long-beard; Odin.
Loni; a dwarf.
Lord of the Host; Odin.
Lord of goats; Lord of the goat's wain, Thor.
Lout; son of Thrall.
Lumpy-leggy; daughter of Thrall.
Lustful; son of Thrall.
Magni; a God, son of Thor.
Maker; Odin.
Maid; daughter of Churl.
Masked One; Odin.
Mead (the)Soul-stirrer; the song-mead.
Mead-drinker; a dwarf.
Mead-wolf; a dwarf.
Meili; a God; Thor's brother.
Memory; a raven.
Menglöd; a giantess or Goddess wooed by Day-spring.
Middle Earth; humanities dwelling, the Earth.
Might; a Valkyrie.
Mightiest God; Odin.
Mighty Weaver; a giant who competes with Odin.
Mimir; a giant guardian of the well of wisdom.
Mimir's Tree; Yggdrasil.
Mist; a Valkyrie.
Mist-blind; a Jötun.
Mist-hel; home of the dead.
Mjöllnir; Thor's hammer.
Modi; Angry, son of Thor.
Mogthrasir; Son-craver, a Jötun.
Moin; a serpent.
Moon; [a male God.]
Moon-hater; a wolf.
Moonless Plains; Fells, regions of the underworld.
Mother; mother of Earl.

Mover of the Handle; father of Moon.
Much-wise; a giant Odin.
Munin; a raven=Memory.
Murk-wood; through which the Sons of Fire ride to Ragnarok.
Nabbi; a dwarf.
Nali; a dwarf.
Nanna; a kinswoman (relative) of Ottar.
Narfi; son of Loki.
Neighbor; son of Churl.
New-counsel; a dwarf.
New-moon; a dwarf.
Night; personification of night.
Nimble-snatcher; one of Aeigir's serving men.
Niping; a dwarf.
Njord; a God, a hostage from the Wanes, (son of)=Frey.
Noatun; Njord's home.
Nokkvir; father of Nanna.
Nori; a dwarf.
Norr; father of Night.
North; a dwarf.
Nyr; a dwarf.
Oaken-peggy; daughter of Thrall.
Oaken-shield; a dwarf.
Oak-thorn; a buck.
Odin; the God. (See also All-father, Bale-worker, Counsellor, Dazzler of Hel, Deathfather, Dread One, Eager in War, Equal-ranked, Father of Beings, Father of Hosts, Father of Men, Father of Spells, Fickle, Flaming-eyed, Flashing-eyed, Grey-beard, Grimnir, Helm-bearer, High One, Hood-winker, Jalk, Keeler, Longbeard, Maker, Masked One, Mightiest God, Much-wise, On-driver, On-rider, On-thruster, Riddle-reader, Rindr, Sage, Shaker, Shape-shifter, Sigrani, Singer (the great),

Slender, Soother, Sooth-sayer, Stormer, Third-highest, Thror, Thund, Tree-rocker, True, Utterer of Gods, Veiled One, Wafter, Wanderer, War-father, War-wanting, Watcher, Wave, Way-wanting, Weaver, Well-comer, Wile-wise, Wind-roar, Wise, Wish-giver, Wizard.)

Odin's brother's; Vili and Ve.
Odin's son; =Baldr.
Odin's son; =Thor.
Odin's sons; the chosen warriors.
Odin's son; Vali.
Olmod; a kinsman of Ottar.
Onar; a dwarf.
On-driver; On-rider, On-thruster, Odin.
Ori; a dwarf, builder of Menglöd's hall.
Ormt; a river.
Osmund; a giant?
Osolf; a hero of Ottar's line.
Ottar; Freyja's lover.
Pale-hoof; a horse.
Peaceful; one of Menglöd's handmaidens.
Peasant; son of Churl.
Pine-needle; a grove.
Plains of Moisture; the surface of the earth?
Powers; High Powers, the Gods [and Goddesses.]
Race-giant; a horse.
Radbard; a hero of Harald Wartooth's line.
Ragnarok; [doom of the Gods, end of this world.]
Ran; one of Odin's wives?
Randver; a hero of Harald Wartooth's line.
Ratatosk; the squirrel gnawing Yggdrasil.
Rati; an awl.
Ravener; a wolf, n.
Regin; a dwarf.

Reifnir; a berserk.
Riddle-reader; Odin.
Rig; =Heimdal.
Rind; a giantess.
Rindr; Odin as husband of Rind.
Roaring-kettle; a spring, where the rivers of Hel flow.
Rover of Air; Loki.
Ruler; father of Erna.
Runes (the); [transcendent Teutonic symbols.]
Saga; a Goddess, wife of Odin.
Sage; Odin.
Samsey; an island.
Sand-strewer; one of Heimdal's mothers.
Sandy-realms; home of dwarfs.
Sea-farer; one of Ottar's forefathers.
Sea-God; Aegir.
Sea-king; one of Ottar's forefathers.
Sea-lover; a giant.
Serpent (the); the World-serpent, son of Loki.
Serpent-slayer; Thor.
Shaker; Odin.
Shall; one of the Norns.
Shape-shifter; Odin.
Sheaf-beard; son of Churl.
Shelterer (the); Yggdrasil.
Sheltering Spirit; one of Menglöd's maidens.
Sheltering-grove; a wood, the refuge of Sun.
She-wolf; one of Heimdal's mothers.
Shield-fierce; a Valkyrie.
Shield of Men; Thor.
Shielding-giants; one of Menglöd's maidens.
Shiner; a horse.
Shining-mane; the horse of Day.
Shrieker; a Valkyrie.

Sif; wife of Thor.
Sigrani; Odin.
Sigmund; son of Volsung.
Sigtrygg; a warrior slain by Halfdan.
Sigurd; son of Sigmund, slayer of Fafnir.
Sigyn; wife of Loki.
Silvery-lock; a horse.
Sinewy; a horse.
Singer (the great); Odin.
Sinmara; a giantess.
Skadi; daughter of the giant Thiazi, wife of Njord.
Skafid; a dwarf.
Skekkil; a kinsman of Ottar.
Skidbladnir; a ship.
Skirfir; a dwarf.
Skilfings; a mythical Folk.
Skirnir; Prey's servant.
Skjoldungs,; a mythical Folk born of Skjold.
Skoll; a wolf.
Skrymir; a giant (=Fjalar).
Skurhild; daughter of Skekkil.
Skybright; a goat.
Slayer of Jötuns; Slayer of Rockgiants, Thor.
Sleep-thorn; grandfather of Menglöd.
Sleipnir; Odin's horse.
Slender; daughter of Churl, Odin.
Sluggard; son of Thrall.
Smith; son of Churl.
Solblind; [Sun-blind] a dwarf?
Son; son of Earl.
Son of Earth; Thor.
Soother; Odin, a serpent.
Soothsayer; Odin.
Sooty-black; a boar, n.

Sooty-face; a cook, n.
Sooty-flame; a cauldron, n.
Sorrow-seed; a Jötun, grandfather of Winter.
Sorrow-whelmer; one of Heimdal's mothers.
Soul-stirrer; the song-mead.
Sound-home; Thiazi's dwelling.
Sounding-clanger; the barrier in front of Menglöd's hall.
South; a dwarf.
Sparkler; a dwarf, forger of treasures.
Speaker; son of Churl.
Spear-fierce; a Valkyrie.
Spear-point; a Valkyrie.
Spring-cold; father of Wind-cold (Day-spring).
Steerer of barks; Thor.
Storm-God; Thor.
Storm-pale; a hawk.
Stormer; Odin.
Stormy-billow; the river from which Ymir was formed.
Strand of corpses; a region in Hel.
Stray-singer; a poet.
Strength-maiden; a Valkyrie.
Strength-wielder; Thor.
Stout; son of Thrall.
Stubbly-beard; son of Churl.
Stumpy; son of Thrall.
Successor; son of Earl.
Summer; personification of summer.
Sun; a Goddess.
Sun-bright; father of Day-spring.
Surt; a fire-giant.
Suttung; a giant, owner of the song-mead.
Svafa; mother of Hildigunn, of Ottar's line.
Svarang; a water-giant.
Sviur; a dwarf.

THE FORMING VERSES

Swadilfari; a mare, mother of Sleipnir.
Swan the Red; ancestor of Ottar.
Swart-head; father of all sorcerers.
Sweet-south; father of Summer.
Swordsman; watchman of the giants.
Tatter-coat; daughter of Churl.
Tender; one of Menglöd's maidens.
Thane; son of Churl.
Thekk; a dwarf.
Thialfi; Thor's servant.
Thiazi; a Jötun-father of Skadi.
Third Highest; Rindr.
Thokk; a witch.
Thor, the God; [See also Father of Wrath, Lord of goats, Lord of the goat's wain, Odin's son, Serpent-slayer, Shield of men, Slayer of Jötuns, Slayer of Rock-giants, Son of Earth, Steerer of barks, Storm-God, Strength-wielder, Thunderer, Warder, Winged Thunder.]
Thora; wife of Dag, mother of many heroes.
Thorin; a dwarf.
Thorir Iron-shield; a berserk.
Thram; a dwarf.
Thrall; father of the thralls Folk.
Thror; Odin, a dwarf.
Thrudgelm; a Jötun, son of Ymir.
Thrym; a Jötun, who stole Thor's hammer.
Thund; Odin.
Thunderer; Thor.
Thunder-flood; a river, n.
Tind; a berserk.
Tree (the); Yggdrasil [the World Tree.]
Tree-rocker; Odin.
Troth-Goddess; of oaths and plightings.
True; Odin.

Tyr; God of war [justice, and heroic glory.]
Tyrfing; a berserk.
Ull; a God.
Uncooled-realm; a region in Jötunheim.
Uni; one of the builders of Menglöd's hall.
Uri; one of the builders of Menglöd's hall.
Utterer of Gods; Odin.
Valas; Wise Women.
Vala-shelf; home of one of the Gods, Odin?
Valgrind; the gates of Valhöll, n.
Valhöll; Odin's dwelling.
Vali; a God, son of Odin and Rind, son of Loki.
Valkyries; Odin's war-maidens.
Var; one of the builders of Menglöd's hall.
Ve; brother of Odin.
Vegdrasil; one of the builders of Menglöd's hall.
Veiled One; Odin.
Vidar; a God, son of Odin.
Vigg; a dwarf.
Vili; brother of Odin.
Vimur; a river.
Virfir; a dwarf.
Vit; a dwarf.
Volsungs; the Folk born of Volsung.
Wafter; Odin.
Wand-elf; a dwarf.
Wanderer; Odin.
Wanes; a line of the Gods.
Wane-home; land of the Wanes.
Waneling; son of a Wane, here Frey, son of Njord.
Waning-moon; a dwarf.
War; a Valkyrie.
War-father; Odin, (son of) =Vidar.
War-fetter; a Valkyrie.

THE FORMING VERSES

War-path; the battle-field at Ragnarok.
War-wanting; Odin.
Warder; Thor.
Wary-wise; a warrior.
Watcher; Odin.
Watchman of Gods; Heimdal.
Wave; Odin.
Way-wanting; Odin.
Weaver; Odin, a serpent.
Weird (Wyrd); one of the three Norns.
Well-comer; Odin.
West; a dwarf.
Whiner; daughter of Thrall.
Wielder; a dwarf.
Wife; daughter of Churl.
Wile-wise; Odin.
Wind-cold; Dayspring.
Wind-cool; father of Winter.
Wind-elf; a dwarf.
Wind-home; home of the sons of Vili and Ve, in the New World.
Window-Shelf; Odin's seat.
Wind-roar; Odin,.
Winged-thunder; Thor.
Winter; personification of winter.
Wise; Odin.
Wise-counsel; a dwarf.
Wise Ones; Menglöd's maidens.
Wish-giver; Odin.
Witch; a giantess, ? daughter of Frost-bringer. Golden-draught.
Wizard; Odin.
Woe-bringer; a giantess, mother of Fenrir.
Wolf (the); Fenrir, n.

Wolf; great-grandfather of Ottar.
Wolf-cubs; sons of Dag.
Wolf the Gaper; a berserk.
Woman; a daughter of Churl.
Wood-home; Vidar's home.
Wood-snake; a cock.
World-serpent; the encircler of the world, son of Loki. [See also Girdle.]
Wounding-wand; the mistletoe.
Yari; a dwarf.
Yelper; one of Heimdal's mothers, a giantess, daughter of Geirrod.
Yeoman; son of Churl.
Yewdale, home of Ull.
Yggdrasil; the World-tree. See also Fate-tree.
Yngvi; a dwarf.
Ymir; the first-born of Jötuns. See also Clay-giant.
Ynglings; a line descended from Yng.
Yngvi; a dwarf.
Youth; son of Churl, son of Earl.

KEYS TO THE TRANSLATORS NOTES

List of Abbreviations
Alv. Alvissmal: The Wisdom of All-wise
Bdr. Baldrs Draumar: Baldr's Dreams
Fj. Fjolsvinnismal: Menglöd
Gg. Grougaldr: Day Spring
Grm. Grimnismal: The Sayings of Grimnir in Torment
Hav. Havamal: The Words of Odin, the High One
Hdl. Hyndluljop: The Lay of Hyndla
Hrbl. Harbarpsljop:Greybeard and Thor
Hym. Hymiskvipa: The Lay of Hymir
Ls. Lokasenna: Loki's Mocking
Rp. Rigspula: The Song of Rig
Skm. Skirnismal: The Story of Skirnir
Vm. Vafprupnismal: The Words of the Mighty Weaver
Vsp. Voluspa: The Wise Womans Prophecy
Prk. Prymskvipa: The Lay of Thrym

Texts and Translations
B. S. Bugge, "Saemundar Edda hins fropa" (Christiania, 1867). Text.
Bm. F. W. Bergmann, Hrbl. (Strassburg, 1872), Gg. and Fj. (1874), Bdr: (1875), Rp. and Hdl. (1876), Hav. (1877), Alv., prk., Hym., Ls. (1878). Text (greatly emended) and translation.
C. Vigfusson and York Powell, "Corpus Poeticum Boreale " (Oxford, 1883). Text and translation.
D. F. E. C. Dietrich, "Altnordisches Lesebuch " (Leipzig, 1864). Text, selections.
Dt. & HI. F. Detter and R. Heinzel, " Saemundar Edda," vol. I (Leipzig, 1903). Text.
E. L. Etmuller, " Altnord. Lesebuch" (Zurich, 1861). Text, selections.
F. H. S. Falk, "Oldnorsk Laesebog" (Christiania, 1889). Text, selections.
F. Magn. F. Magnusen, "Den aeldere Edda, etc." (1821-23). Text.

G H. Gering, "Die Lieder der alteren Edda" (Padeborn, 1904). Text.
    H. Gering, "Die Edda" (Leipzig, 1892). Translation.
H. K Hildebrand, "Lieder der alteren Edda" (Padeborn, 1876). Text.
Hold. A. Holder and A. Holtzmann (Leipzig, 1875). Text and translation.
H. A. Heusler, "Voluspa" (Berlin, 1887). Text and translation.
J. Finnur Jonsson, "Saemundar Edda" (Reykjavik, 1905). Text.
K. Copenhagen Edition (1787-1828).
L. H. Luning, "Die Edda" (Zurich, 1859). Text.
M. P. A. Munch, "Den aeldere Edda" (Christiania, 1847). Text.
Mb. Th. Mobius, "Edda Saemundar" (Leipzig, 1860). Text.
R. Rask, "Edda Saemundar" (Stockholm, 1818).
S. B. Sijmons, "Die Lieder der Edda" (Halle, 1888), vol. 2. Text.
Simr. K. Simrock, "Die Edda, die altere u. die jungere" (Stuttgart, 1882). Translation.
Th. B. Thorpe, "The Edda of Saemund the Learned" (London, 1866). Translation.
W. L. Wimmer, "Oldnordisk Laesebog" (Copenhagen, 1889). Text, selections.

NEW GLOSSARY

Assembly (Althing); the annual Heathen Free Assembly of the Viking age; an ancient Teutonic predecessor of the modern republic and of individual representation today.

Berserker: Heathen warrior who fights with unchained fury.

Blessing (Blot): The symbolic and spiritual act of invoking the Holy Powers by the sprinkling of water from an evergreen sprig, by the Hammer Sign, or by other acts for the benefit of the Folk and for the consecration of Holy places and objects.

Disir (Mother Spirits): Revered maternal protective Deities.

Einherjar: Lone Heathen fighter, or single combatant. In Eddaic lore; one who has died fighting valiantly on the battlefield and is taken to the Halls of Vallhala to await the final conflict with the Opposing Powers.

Ethno-cultural: In the modern Heathen sense; the all-encompassing system of Teutonic cultural values and spirituality, forming a biological link with its members and descendants everywhere, both collectively and individually.

Ethno-linguistic (Cultural linguistics): the scientific analysis of the relationship between languages and cultures. Jacob Grimm, the German philologist and founder of Grimm's Law of linguistics, traced the elements of a historical, common Teutonic religion by identifying shared Teutonic language related associations, in an 1835 work that remains influential today; *Teutonic Mythology*.

Faith: A monotheistic device that enables belief by the acceptance of a doctrine without proof, rather than from trust in a reality that can either be demonstrated naturally or perceived intuitively from one's own ethno-cultural values.

Fetch (Fylgja): The attending spiritual being, animal or symbolic, that follows along a Heathens life path.

Folk (The): Ethnically related Teutonic Heathens who uphold the Holy Powers and the primal values of the Teutonic Nations and their descendants wherever they may live. This may extend to Heathens of other ethno-cultures.

Germanic Neopaganism: Newly reconstructed Heathenism, honoring the Northern Way much as our ancestors did; drawing upon rediscovered knowledge, an evolving world view, and the Runes. Authoritarianism, universalism, and new-age paganism are largely rejected, while an emphasis is placed on traditions grounded within our shared Teutonic heritage. Modern Heathenism is focused more upon evolving forward the primal, honorable values and sacred beliefs that are supported by the historical record, than with personality cults, esoteric mysteries, and poetic embellishments.

Heathen: "Heath-Dweller." (Similar to *Pagan,* from the Latin *Pagani*, meaning "country dweller.") One of the indigenous Teutonic Folk or their descendants who recognizes the Holy Powers *(Poly*theism) and the Opposing Powers, and who may or may not distinguish a higher Holy Power beyond the mortal Holy Powers. Contrast with *Pan*theism (esp. as found in Wiccan Paganism), and *Mono*theism.

Hammer Sign: The symbolic affirmation of Thor's hammer.

Heathen Holy Times: Honoring feasts, loosely held around the two solstices and the two equinoxes; **Easter** (Ostara) in Spring, **Midsummer**, **Harvest** in Fall, **Yuletide** in Winter.

Hel (Place): Abode or halls of the dead; a neutral place in the afterlife where Folk may continue to evolve. (Compare with the Christian *Hell*; a place of eternal damnation and torture.)

THE FORMING VERSES

Holy Powers (The): Elder Kin. The revered Spiritual Forces of the Teutonic Folk; Gods, Goddesses, and Ancestors.

Holy Power (The): The immortal Holy Power that stands above the mortal Holy Powers. God.

Northern Way (The): [As defined by Wolf Wickham.] Teutonic Heathenism, or the Northern Way, is founded upon the honorable values of a Kindred Folk:

- **Foundations.** A belief in and a reverence for; 1.) The Holy Power(s), the concepts of the World Tree, and the Runes. 2.) Individual liberty freely united with a Kindred loyalty. 3.) The realization that there is perpetual war between the Holy Powers and the Opposing Powers, in which we are an active part of here on earth, and in the next life.
- **Principles.** 1.) The Holy Powers are divided, imperfect, and evolving, and we are the descendants and kin of these forces. 2.) Evolution of the individual and of the Folk are towards higher, noble ideals based upon constructive will, knowledge, and balance. 3.) The Life Force manifest by the Holy Powers is divine, as it is within the noble Folk. 4.) There is an afterlife and a reckoning, with a continuing evolution or self-transformation. 5.) The life path of the Folk and the folkish individual is a struggle against the Opposing Powers of the universe.
- **Aims.** 1.) The assimilation of the Teutonic individual, family, and Kindred back into the Northern Way through a missionary movement. 2.) The reconstruction and restoration of the Northern Way into robust, modern and evolving, independent Kindred's. 3.) The creation of trans-national Kindred's within a Teutonic Free Assembly.

Norns: Three female Deities who influence the path of life; Urd (what has become), Verdandi (what is), and Skuld (what is *likely* to become.) Evolving forces in the web of existence.

Opposing Powers (The) or Forces: The challenging and/or dark and destructive forces recognized by the Teutonic Folk.

Reverence: Heathens *stand with* the Holy Powers in reverence, out of the same love, honor, and respect given to one's immediate family and Folk, and will fight to preserve Kindred values, in this life and the next. (See Worship.)

Runes (Teutonic Symbols): The hidden, identified and revealed through transformative symbols, leading to a higher knowledge of reality. A letter symbol of the Norse "alphabet" or *futhark* that has both phonetic value and a profoundly transcendent concept association. Runic realization encompasses form, ideation, and measure—as a potential vehicle for divination and absolute perception.

Tree of Life (Yggdrasil): The all-encompassing concepts and realms of Heathenism embodied in the living Tree of the Folk. The evolutionary map of Teutonic Heathenism.

Worship: In the Judaic, Christian, and Muslim monotheist faiths the jealous God is the omnipotent Lord and Master who owns all of His creations, including humanity, demanding absolute surrender, servitude, and adoration under the threat of eternal damnation. (See Reverence.)

Wyrd (Weird): Primal layer. The personal and transformative web of reality in time and space. On an everyday level; the present that is unfolding from the past. Also related to the greater concept of **Orlog,** from Ur; beyond law.

Valkyries: Fierce female spirits, warrior maidens of Odin.

www.ingramcontent.com/pod-product-compliance
Lightning Source LLC
Chambersburg PA
CBHW031447040426
42444CB00007B/1010